CRITICAL WRITING
for the JOURNALIST

―――――――◆―――――――

ROLAND E. WOLSELEY

School of Journalism, Syracuse University

CHILTON COMPANY — BOOK DIVISION
Publishers

Philadelphia   *New York*

LIBRARY OF CONGRESS CATALOG CARD NUMBER 59-6095

MANUFACTURED IN THE UNITED STATES OF AMERICA
BY QUINN & BODEN COMPANY, INC., RAHWAY, N. J.

Preface

This book grew from the needs of both teacher and students in a class in critical writing for journalism. Those volumes available dealt with only one area of criticism—literature—except for a single instance embracing several of the arts that was outdated and out of print.

I do not pretend to have evolved a theory of criticism, journalistic or otherwise. Neither have I attempted to exhaust the many theories, philosophies, and methods of criticism. This would be impossible in any work short of an encyclopedia. Instead, I have tried to set down the facts about journalistic criticism, as practiced in the United States today, that I believe to be helpful to would-be critics, to new critics, and to experienced critics interested in other methods or viewpoints, as well as to readers and listeners who would understand journalistic criticism and its problems.

This book, then, lays no great claims to originality. One may be its plan, which is to outline some general principles of critical writing in journalism, to examine such work as an occupation, and then to explain and provide guidance in the preparation for journalistic use of various kinds of critical material dealing with the fine and popular arts. This approach has been tested in the classroom as well as in the professional field.

Justification for the studying of criticism of all the arts in combination is found in an observation made more than half a century ago by C. T. Winchester, one of the classic writers on the subject. In his *Principles of Literary Criticism,* after defining criticism as "the intelligent appreciation of any work of art, and by consequence the just estimate of its value and rank," he adds:

"Literary criticism is, of course, concerned only with literature; but the general nature of the functions of criticism is much the same whether the object criticized be literature, or painting, or sculpture, or music."

Another aspect of this book that may be original (at least quantitatively) is its report on the place and the nature of journalistic criticism. Aside from an occasional chapter in a journalism textbook, little attempt has been made to describe and evaluate journalistic criticism in this country. Instead, we generally have been given guidance on reporting news of the arts rather than help on reviewing and criticizing the arts themselves. Journalistic criticism, in fact, so often has been the object of sneers by academic critics and by many a practicing artist—often with entire justice—that to attempt to consider it seriously may seem merely defensive. This book is no defense. It seeks, however, to find out why journalistic criticism often is inadequate, to show that there is more competent critical writing being produced than apparently is realized, and to suggest methods of improvement.

The author knows full well that fundamental to first-rate criticism is a thorough knowledge of the history, the techniques, and the practitioners of the art under consideration. It is, of course, impossible for one or perhaps any book to impart this knowledge. Certainly all a volume of the present length can be expected to do is to cover briskly the subjects listed in its table of contents. No one person can master all the arts. In this complex and swiftly moving world, mastery of even one is too much for most of us. Thus there is no attempt here to brief the critic on the fine and popular arts themselves. He must school himself at this point.

Oliver Jensen, of the *American Heritage* magazine, during a panel discussion at a Magazine Publishers Association meeting in 1958, said: "We see, we think, we hope for signs of a cultural explosion in the United States." He found support for hope in certain facts: that New York museum attendance recently had been three times that at baseball stadia and that "the paper backs of good books by authors like Plato and Aristotle are doing enormously well." He thinks, he said, that "we can aspire to a higher level of writing . . . I think we have to lead . . . I think it's terribly important not to just follow and not to just try to find out what people want and give it to them. . . ."

When this cultural explosion is set off, the media of mass communication must be ready. It is not the ingrown scholars applying ephemeral aesthetic theories, able to communicate mainly with each other and rarely with the public, who will be of direct help to the ordinary citizen at that time. The burrowing scholars have an indispensable place, but it is not in the popular press in direct contact with the mass of the people. It is the cultural guidance to be found in the several realms of journalism—the reviewers and critics, who scarcely think of themselves as guides—that will keep critical journalism abreast of what is occurring in society.

Is it not traditionally the function of the press to inform, guide, and influence? The arts, as Carl Grabo has said so well, "are not only a source of pleasure but a means to knowledge, and a guide to action."

Specifically, this book aims to help the critic himself to:

Realize the full extent of his responsibility,

Learn how to apply basic principles of criticism to his work,

Remain aware of his readers' or listeners' needs, but go beyond these to assist them in forming their tastes.

Be an increasingly effective writer of critical material for journalism.

ROLAND E. WOLSELEY

Syracuse, New York

Acknowledgments

Many former students and other friends now doing critical writing have been generous in providing many different kinds of assistance. The author thanks them all, as well as those publishers who have permitted him to reproduce illustrations and quotations; these are credited with their contributions.

In particular he extends thanks to the following for their willingness to discuss ideas, read chapters, provide examples, or aid in other ways:

Miss Nevart Apikian, motion-picture critic of the Syracuse (N. Y.) *Post-Standard;* Mrs. Carolyn Jane Avery, a free-lance writer in Tempe, Arizona; Milton R. Bass, critic of many of the arts for the Pittsfield (Mass.) *Berkshire Eagle;* Robert Berkvist, of the staff of the New York *Times Book Review;* James W. Carty, Jr., of the Nashville *Tennessean* staff; Miss Anne Marie Duval, reviewer and reporter for the Schenectady (N. Y.) *Union-Star;* Donald Freeman, radio-television editor of the San Diego *Union* and syndicated columnist for the Copley News Service; Donald D. Key, art and music critic of the Cedar Rapids (Iowa) *Gazette;* Robert C. Marsh, music critic of the Chicago *Sun-Times;* William D. Patterson, associate publisher of *The Saturday Review* and director of its syndicate; Mrs. Ruth E. Riley, formerly a reviewer for the Kansas City (Kans.) *Kansan;* Prof. Robert W. Root, one of my colleagues at Syracuse University; Miss Evelyn Smith, journalism librarian, Syracuse University; Robert L. Sokolsky, entertainment editor, Syracuse *Herald-Journal* and *Herald-American;* Mrs. Aline Jean Treanor, art critic, Oklahoma City *Daily Oklahoman;* and Claude Callaway, Carlton Frazier, Mort Hochstein, Mrs. Elaine Stryker Spear, and John H. Sorenson.

To my wife, Bernice, a special note of thanks for her as always invaluable editorial work.

Contents

Preface vii

1. What Is Critical Writing? 1

2. Extent and Functions 13

3. The Criticisms of Journalistic Criticism 25

4. As an Occupation 37

5. Background for Criticism 55

6. The Philosophies of Criticism 70

7. The Critic's Style 86

8. Writing Reviews 99

9. Writing the Critical Article 130

10. Writing Syndicated Criticism 163

11. Handling Special Pages and Sections 176

12. The Critical Journals 189

Selected Bibliography 197

Index 201

What Is Critical Writing?

The beginning journalistic critic, the club and church reporter, perhaps, suddenly assigned by the city desk to substitute for the ailing movie reviewer, is in no mood to ponder the query heading this chapter. His first questions are more likely to be: "How do I do this job?" and "What do I know about this movie?", followed by a rush to the files to gather tips from the work of the regular writer.

Similarly, the veteran and skilled reviewer for a distinguished literary monthly gives little time to pondering "What is critical writing?" He no more dwells on this question than does a great architect on "What is architecture?" as he designs a new building.

Then why should we, at the outset, consider this evidently abstract and philosophical question? There are good reasons. One is that having a satisfactory answer helps a critic to know what he is doing and to do a better job. Another is that many of the noted critics, journalistic and otherwise, seem at one time or another to have been troubled by the question and to have worked out their own answers (as, for example, George Saintsbury, Matthew Arnold, W. D. Howells, and George Bernard Shaw). The neophyte must someday resolve the problem if he is to continue to be a critic and to achieve effectiveness. The expert critic has settled it, although he may at various times arrive at different answers.

Making a Distinction

Before any answers are given, as the history of criticism reveals them, however, it is necessary to repeat here (since prefaces often are left unread) that this book deals only with a particular type

1

of criticism—journalistic. The flippant reader is likely to say that criticism is criticism, and that's that. He sees only good or bad criticism, possibly. But there is a valid distinction between the critical writing that appears in newspapers and magazines of general circulation and that which appears in certain scholarly journals and books.

Usually the critic for journalism cannot write criticism for the specialists in aesthetics or for the classical scholars of any of the fine arts (the popular arts seem not, so far, to have commanded much serious scholarship). And the reverse is true. So far as the general public is concerned, the erudite critics of literature make no sense; these scholars cannot or do not care to master the art of popular communication. They have invented a specialized language, much as sociologists, economists, psychologists, and other social as well as natural scientists have developed a professional and necessary argot. The journalistic critic, on the other hand, dare not use such jargon even if he can, for it severs him from his readers. These groups should complement each other, but, because of the sneers of some of the nonjournalistic critics over the years, enmity has developed between them.

Said the novelist Robert Ruark, most of whose career has been in journalism: "I haven't got a good deal of respect for the garden variety of reviewers. They're full of the stock clichés of the public relations fellows."

Wrote Geoffrey Wagner, a novelist and English teacher, in *The American Scholar* during 1957: "There are, alas, only a very few fortunate individuals who can combine, with the grace of a Lionel Trilling or a Harry Levin, the arts of criticism and reviewing. But it is this kind of critic, rather than the hack reviewman who is presently working for the large Sunday media, who has a deep love for the 'craft of fiction.'"

"Literary critics . . . range from the journalistic reviewers discussing three or four books a day to the dignified, careful critic who, with a background of culture and learning, passes judgment on movements and tendencies in the large," says a widely used reference book (Thrall and Hibbard, *A Handbook to Literature*). This volume adds: "The first type gave cause for Disraeli's charge:

'You know who critics are?—the men who have failed in literature and art.' "

The exact nature and the merits of the criticism (including praise) made of journalistic critics are taken up later. Here we echo these adverse remarks only to help us understand what kind of criticism is expected of the journalistic critic—not only what is expected of him, but also what it is reasonable for him to expect to produce.

The Area Defined

Critical writing, in present-day American journalism, is the writing of essays and articles for publication and material for oral delivery that appreciates and judges the arts.

Certain words in this definition need close examination. *Present-day* is used because we do not want to be responsible for different concepts of critical writing that may have been held in the past but are no longer used. It also focuses attention on what is happening in our own time.

American is used because journalism is an international activity and not because of any chauvinistic attitude. We cannot hold ourselves responsible here for thorough examination of journalistic criticism as practiced in other nations.

An *essay* is a short prose discussion of a limited topic or subject.

An *article* somewhat resembles the essay but frequently is longer, and it differs in purpose, usually being intended to convince, entertain, or inform, whereas in our time the few essays being written are personal and informal.

Appreciates means having a clear perception of the aesthetic qualities of an object. Once the primary purpose of critical writing, it is now a declining function of such composition. Yet it survives, as a glance at the little literary magazines shows, and in the pure sense it deserves to.

Judges is used here as a synonym for evaluates; i.e., to pass judgment upon or to indicate the value of a work of art. This function will be explored in great detail in later chapters, for it is fundamental to a critic and has undergone considerable alteration over the years.

The *arts* judged by the journalistic critic fall into two groups, the fine and the popular. The fine arts, of course, are literature (including poetry), the dance, painting (including drawing), sculpture, architecture, music, and the drama; the popular arts, still being debated as to whether they are arts at all, are motion pictures, radio, television, recordings, and photography.

What Critical Writing Is Not

Critical writing for journalism is not news reports of art shows, gossip of stage and screen and television stars, and chitchat about the book world. These all are forms of journalism, to be sure, but they are not critical writing, which concentrates on the result of the artists' efforts. It does not neglect the artist personally. But the focus is more on his work than on him. They cannot be separated, of course, but a personality sketch does not serve as a substitute for a critical article. One learns little about architecture from reading such facts about Frank Lloyd Wright as his age, the place of his birth, and the titles of his books. Even an elaborate description of his personal appearance has little place in a volume on architecture.

Nor is critical writing that type of journalism known as feature writing. Features may be about artists and about their work, but they are not intended to serve as critical guides. They may give us art history, biographies of artists, personality sketches, and human interest side lights on the arts, but they are not critical writing. A radio or television interview with an artist might be called art news, if he reveals something new about himself or his work, but it is not ordinarily an evaluation.

Confusion comes about because, in American journalism, art editors, literary editors, music critics, and movie reviewers, to name a few, are expected to do several jobs at once. Take a music editor: he must review all the concerts, recitals, and other music performances of consequence or interest in the community. He must print the news of local musical developments: the formation of a new club, a professional change in the career of a widely known musical figure in the city, the opening of new music schools or studios or the offering of new courses by the school of music of a nearby college or university. In most areas he must give much attention to the commercial side: the opening of a new music store, the installation of a line of records and sheet music in a local department store. On a large publication he can delegate certain of these chores, but on a small one he must do them all himself. The music editor and the music critic, therefore, are often very different types of journalists, although both are journalists. The critic is the writer in a truer sense of the word.

Types of Composition

Whether he spends some of his time on other types of journalism or not, the critic needs to understand critical writing and what goes into it. It should be clear to him that all types of composition are used in such writing, except invented narration. Description, exposition, and argumentation naturally are emphasized. A critic who does not know what to say in judging what he is looking at or listening to properly resorts to simply describing it (reporting). He is a wise critic if not an effective one (at this point, in fact, he is no critic at all). He also is rare if he makes this decision, for most journalistic critics are not content when in such a dilemma to be thus modest but too often try to take a position and exercise a judgment for which they do not have the critical equipment.

Narrative also is used, but it is actual, not imagined. It may be a critic's story of his encounter with an author or a dancer or of his own experience in the same area as that of the art he is criticizing (a travel book reviewer can use narrative effectively, for instance). Unless he signals to his reader that he is fictionizing, however, the critic should not break over into the story form that does not rest in fact.

Critical Thinking

Llewellyn Jones, when he was literary editor of the Chicago *Evening Post's Friday Literary Review,* a tabloid section much like the *Books* of the New York *Herald Tribune,* used to insist that the study of critical writing began with the study of language. His point makes the nature of critical writing more clear.

He wrote in his book on book reviewing: "When the specialist in biology writes a book to prove that society at large is a biological organism subject to certain laws of growth and decay, the critic need not compete with the author in detailed knowledge of biology, but he ought to know enough about society—if not by book, then by his own participation in it—to challenge the biologist's assumptions, the challenge being either in terms of history or of social psychology."

So the competent critic, Mr. Jones thought, knows one subject in detail and knows everything else in perspective. Perspective he calls "the framework into which everything else fits." He refers to Alfred North Whitehead's term "mental climate," meaning the general state of ideas current at a given time. Mr. Jones illustrated by referring to Prof. Baker Brownell, author of *The Human Community* and many other books, who, while teaching philosophy and journalism at Northwestern University, lectured on the Einstein theory of relativity, with the aid of scientists from the rest of the faculty. He did not attempt to explain the theory in detail but tried to give his students a general idea of Einstein's contribution. After that, when the students heard the term "fourth dimension," they were in a position to recognize it as a scientific or philosophical concept known to the mathematical world.

Thereafter, if they are given for review a book in which the fourth dimension is presented as an element in the world of spiritualism or a discovery of the previous week, they immediately realize that the author does not know what he is talking about.

The climate of opinion shifts so swiftly that by the time this book is published the following illustration may be inexact. In 1952 or 1953, if a Russian dance company had succeeded in coming to the United States at all, it is likely that the group's appearance would have caused a riot. But in 1958 the Moiseyev Dancers' performance at the Metropolitan Opera House in New York was one of the artistic sensations of the season and won rave notices from critics and ovations from packed audiences. The reaction of the critics might have been the same in 1952 or 1953, because critics—at least the best ones—do not judge a work of art along political or national lines. But, in general, the public is still not capable of preserving its aesthetic sense, as witness the complaints by some parents during the same year in Syosset, Long Island, when their children were expected to sing, among other songs, a Russian ditty praising the city of Moscow. New York City is an international community, and objectors to the dancers could not be heard easily, whereas Syosset is so small that the objectors could make their views known readily.

Just as in other types of journalism, clear thinking helps to produce clear journalistic writing. But the journalistic reviewer must be able to think critically as well as clearly. Critical thinking demands certain mental equipment: a measure of objectivity, realization of the climate of opinion, awareness of the methods of making estimates or arriving at judgments, perspective gained through knowledge of the art of being evaluated, and understanding of the audience. These qualities are not possessed by every journalist, nor can they all necessarily be achieved by any journalist through study and practice. They are qualities that separate the journalistic critic from virtually all his fellows in journalism. Only the editorial writer for the press and the commentator for radio and television must possess similar virtues as a journalist. But even journalists are differentiated by their subject matter, the place of their material in the medium, the public attitude toward their work, and the impact of commercialism upon what they do and where they appear. All this remains for us to explore.

Reviewing and Criticizing

The words *review* and *criticism* have come to be used interchangeably. It probably is hopeless to expect the world of journalism to retain any distinction, valuable as it might be for students of critical writing. The distinction is made here as a contribution to understanding, with full realization that the professional critic may forget it after it has served the purpose of clarifying his thinking.

Literally, a reviewer is not a critic but a reporter who writes what amounts to a follow-up news story about the material viewed or heard. Under the American pattern of journalism, he therefore avoids expression of opinion. He merely reports—that is, describes through the senses without attempting to evaluate or appreciate. This much any journalist above the level of a copy boy can do, for it requires pure reportorial skill instead of critical ability. Such reporting, while not criticism, actually is a component of all journalistic criticism and is one that differentiates it from the classical types of criticism.

The New York *Herald Tribune* gave a clear demonstration of the distinction when it one day assigned a reporter as well as a critic to write about a concert. Their writings were printed side by side. Across the two columns ran a headline reading "Brooklyn Symphony Has Debut." Reading out from it into one column was a subordinate heading: "Reporter's View: A Gala Occasion." Beside it was another readout head saying: "Critic's Review: A Good Beginning."

Here is what the reporter wrote:

By Herbert Kupferberg

Beethoven's Fifth Symphony never sounded as good to Brooklynites as it did last night, when the newly formed Brooklyn Symphony Orchestra played it as the opening number of its first concert at the Brooklyn Academy of Music.

The 2,000 persons in the hall cheered Dr. Herbert Zipper, the conductor, and his eighty-six musicians for five minutes after the symphony, and they cheered between movements, too. As a matter of fact, they cheered for two minutes even before the orchestra began to play. And they kept right on cheering through the rest of the program, which included Strauss's "Till Eulenspiegel" and the fourth act of Verdi's opera, "Don Carlos," sung in costume with Regina Resnik, Brenda Lewis, Oscar Natzka, Frank Gamboni and George Tozzi as soloists.

"This," said Miss Dorothy Kors, a committee woman, as she gazed out at the applauding audience, "is a tremendous success—socially and musically. Look at those judges— Di Giovanna, Livingston, Giaccone, and the rest of them. A whole row of judges! And we have a telegram from Governor Dewey, too."

She was referring to Supreme Court Justices Anthony J. Di Giovanna, Jacob H. Livingston and Francis X. Giaccone, who were in the audience.

Mrs. Lester Miller, co-chairman of the Women's Division, said last night's concert was only a start.

"This is our pilot season," she explained. "Only two concerts—tonight and Sunday afternoon at the Brooklyn Technical High School. But we have great plans and, as they say at Ebbets Field, wait till next year!"

Last night's audience was to Brooklyn what a first-night Metropolitan audience is to New York, except that most of them arrived on time. Some of the people swept into

Reviewing and Criticizing

the hall in evening clothes and some just walked in in regular clothes. During the intermission they went out into the lobby and looked each other over. They all seemed to agree that Dr. Zipper, who used to be the conductor of the Manila Symphony, had done a good job with the orchestra, and they said the singers were good, too.

Francis D. Perkins, music editor of the New York *Herald Tribune,* was accosted in the lobby and asked how this crowd stacked up against other concert crowds for elegance and tone.

"Audiences," replied the hard-bitten Mr. Perkins, "are the same all over—New York, Boston, Philadelphia. It makes no difference."

Criticism, on the other hand, as we have seen, is an expression of opinion about the performance (let us use this word to represent a book, a concert, a recital, a dance, an art show, or some other evidence of an art). Here the journalist goes beyond reporting or reviewing into the realm of the subjective. He moves from the objective to the subjective. Here is the same musical event criticized; the critical words have been italicized in this reproduction.

By Francis D. Perkins

BROOKLYN SYMPHONY ORCHESTRA, Herbert Zipper, conductor, first concert last night at the Brooklyn Academy of Music. The program:

Symphony No. 5, in
   C minor .... Beethoven
Opera, "Don Carlos,"
   Act IV, Part 1....   Verdi
  Elizabeth, Brenda Lewis; Princess of Eboli, Regina Resnik; King Philip II, Oscar Natzka; Rodrigo, Frank Gamboni; Grand Inquisitor, George Tozzi.
Till Eulenspiegel .. Richard Strauss

The new Brooklyn Symphony Orchestra gave the first public performance of a career which, it is hoped, will be a long and distinguished one, last night in the Brooklyn Academy of Music. The program played by the eighty-six musicians under Herbert Zipper's direction was familiar in its strictly instrumental components, and unfamiliar in the operatic excerpt which separated Beethoven's Fifth Symphony and Richard Strauss's "Till Eulenspiegel"; twenty-six years have elapsed since Verdi's "Don Carlos" was last performed at the Metropolitan.

Dr. Zipper, it was stated, heard more than 700 candidates in auditions before making his selections. Judging by the performance of the Beethoven Symphony, the roster *was well chosen.* With Broadus Erle as concert master, the orchestra *gave an impression of thorough technical ability and musicianship* throughout its membership, with *no apparent weak spots* in any particular section. The string tone, after the opening pages, was *well fused and sonorous;* the brass and woodwind tone was of *good quality,* and the performance as a whole was *well unified,* and, with a few exceptions, *praise-*

worthy in the balance of the component instrumental choirs. It reflected marked credit on the conductor's ability as an organizer and trainer; a straight-forward interpretation also told of his technical ability, musicianship, and experience. Considerations of time and transportation denied the reviewer an opportunity to hear the Strauss tonepoem.

The excerpts from "Don Carlos," which included the work's best known arias—Philip's "Ella giammai m'amo!" and the Princess of Eboli's "O don fatale"—were presented in costume and with operatic action; the king's table with its two candles was placed before a screen at the right of the stage. Miss Resnik's *fine* voice, *while sometimes giving a hint of forcing, was employed with convincing dramatic intensity;* Miss Lewis's tones in Elizabeth's music were *pleasing in quality, although lacking consistent firmness.* Mr. Natzka sang much of the opening aria *expressively,* and Frank Gamboni and George Tozzi *fared creditably* as Rodrigo and the Grand Inquisitor, and both the Symphony and the operatic scene were enthusiastically received.

—New York *Herald Tribune*

The difference between reviewing and criticism can be put another way. In the pure and literal sense, it is that the review is the result of objective reporting and the criticism the outcome of subjective reporting. The first reports what goes on outside the reviewer, and the other tells what goes on inside the critic. For a time the Paris edition of the *Herald Tribune* dramatized this regularly by dividing its book reviews into two parts: "The Book" and "The Criticism." These two sections of the review were clearly so marked and the writing was distinctly different.

Most journalistic criticism is an interwoven fabric, with more or less emphasis on one or the other, depending on the perceptivity of the critic, his critical equipment, or what he considers his function to be in relation to the material. Below is a typical example of the combined review-criticism. Note how, in the opening paragraph, the critic, who has a wide following on the Pacific Coast, has not indicated what he thinks of the performance but concentrates on four of the usual journalistic basics (where, when, what, who; why and how, however, are not and cannot be dealt with). Also note that the first paragraph is at least twice as long as it should be for comfortable reading.

By Alfred Frankenstein

San Francisco has had its share of musical premieres over the decades, but no new work ever disclosed here is likely to be repeated with such assurance of success as

Carl Orff's "Carmina Burana," which was given its first American performance Sunday night at the Opera House by Giovanni Camajani and his Schola Cantorum from the University of San Francisco.

(This is followed by about 500 words of historical background on the work itself. Then the reader comes to the estimate of its performance on this particular occasion.)

It is a big, difficult and complex thing for a fairly new chorus to attempt, but Camajani's singers handled it magnificently, and members of the San Francisco Symphony Orchestra also responded magnifi-

cently to Camajani's direction. The soloists—Mario Segale, soprano; Ronald Dutro, baritone; and Gordon Zimmerman, tenor—all carried off their assignments as if they had been singing "Carmina Burana" all their lives.

(The critic then expresses two regrets: "the absence of the text from the printed program" and "all the work that went into this performance was dissipated after one evening," with supporting reasons for these views. The remaining 150 words describe and evaluate other parts of the program.)

—San Francisco *Chronicle*

The value of this distinction between reviewing and criticism for the new writer of critical material is that when he is forced to do a quick job or believes himself insufficiently grounded in the art form he can skip the critical writing and confine himself to the relatively objective reporting and supply his publication with something fair and usable. This noncritical writing in such a circumstance is much to be preferred to baseless and ignorant criticism.

Some of the readers of this book, for instance, cannot understand certain modern paintings or pieces of sculpture. If they were called upon to write critically about an exhibit of such work, they would hardly know what to set down, except that they don't like it, don't understand it, and don't think artists should produce such work. This sort of reaction is neither informed nor intelligent, and should be avoided. But what is to be substituted? If the material is available, say in catalogs or by interview with informed artists or art specialists, the space might better be used in telling the reader something about the artist—his philosophy; his previous exhibits; the comments of others about his work, both pro and con; the number of persons at the exhibit; what else may be seen; and other information that can be obtained by careful inquiry. The reviewer then would be doing no injustice to an artist whose technique and method he has had no opportunity to study and understand.

There are no theories of reviewing as there are theories of criticism, as explained in Chapter 6. The reviewer does his job as does any other newsman. He takes notes on firsthand events. He consults reference books for facts about the artists and their schools. He familiarizes himself with catalogs, asks the artists direct questions, talks to guards and to people at the exhibit, asks the ticket taker or seller for facts about attendance, reports on special events, incidents, or whatever else may make attractive copy, but does not enter the area of criticism. His philosophy of writing is that it must approach objectivity as well as possible, be accurate, complete, and well-rounded. But he is not working as a critic.

The critic, however, cannot stop there. In the portions of his article in which he, too, reports, he must of course meet all the standards of sound reporting. He must spell the artists' names correctly, quote the titles of paintings accurately, and follow all the other rules of acceptable journalistic writing. To all this he adds what converts a report into a criticism: his opinions.

Extent and Functions

Four of the more common opinions about journalistic criticism that may be discovered by putting questions to journalists as well as readers of critical writing are:

1. The number of persons doing critical writing for American mass media as well as for specialized outlets is small.

2. Vast quantities of space are given over to critical writing.

3. No meritorious writing of this type appears outside the press of a few Atlantic seaboard cities, chiefly New York, Washington, Philadelphia, and Boston.

4. No critical writing in the United States, except in a newspaper or two and a handful of highly specialized periodicals, is to be taken seriously as literature, or even as journalism.

The next chapter will examine this last statement, for it is a vital one. If true, this book might just as well not have been written. In this chapter, in seeking to establish the extent and functions of journalistic criticism in the United States, we shall deal with the first three opinions.

The Number of Critical Writers

One clue to the extent of journalistic criticism is the number of persons listed as critics. Statistical information about many aspects of American journalism is sparse and uneven at best. No central listing exists of critics who work for newspapers, magazines, radio and television, news services, and all other media. In fact, only three directories attempt to list such writers —the *Editor & Publisher International Year Book* and *Working Press of the Nation*, Vol. I, which name those in the various arts for daily papers only, and *Literary Market Place*, an annual that lists book critics of newspapers, magazines, and radio programs. Informal lists of book-review lecturers have been issued by publishers' groups but are not easily available.

In no list is a distinction made between an editor and a critic;

"They're critics!"

Courtesy, *The Writer's Digest*

in some, one cannot tell who is a reporter of news of one of the arts and who a critic of that art. Since all these functions often are the responsibility of one person, this is not so serious a fault as to disqualify these records, even though for the meticulous scholar they leave an impression of inexactness.

Without, therefore, making a costly nationwide study, it is impossible to indicate accurately the total number of critics. An approximate figure is available for the daily newspaper press. Beyond this, there are the critics who serve the syndicates, magazines, broadcasting media, and weekly press. In them, as in daily papers, much of the effort is combined with reporting and feature writing.

Scouring of various sources[1] leads to the conclusion that about 2,000 persons make all or a considerable part of their living writing journalistic criticism for newspapers and magazines of general circulation. Most of these are attached to daily papers. How many thousands more, as free lancers or through some slender connection, write criticism for the remaining printed and spoken media is anyone's guess. It is a figure that must run into several more thousands at least, for there are the many writers who prepare critical material voluntarily, receiving, at most, tickets to the theater or movie or a review copy of the book. Whether they are paid in dollars for their work is irrelevant at this moment. What is relevant is that they roll paper into a typewriter and praise or damn a book, painting, or television program, and thereby influence the attitudes of others toward the performance of an art.

A closer look at the number of daily newspaper people who in some sense may be considered critics is in itself, however, an answer to those persons who say offhandedly that the number doing such work is inconsequential. It is important quantitatively as well as qualitatively.

A count of the persons listed as writers or editors of material about the various arts (and we must remember that editors usually, in this case, are writers as well) for dailies alone, gives us this division:

> Art (including sculpture and painting) 260
> Books 450
> Motion pictures 350
> Music 360
> Radio and television 375
> Theater 325

These total an average of more than one to each daily in the United States, because added to them must be others who serve

[1] *Editor & Publisher International Year Book, Newspaper Rates and Data,* Ayer's *Directory of Newspapers and Periodicals, Literary Market Place, Working Press of the Nation, Film Daily Year Book of Motion Pictures.*

as critics of photography and recordings. Duplications have been allowed for; if they had not been, the total would be beyond 3,000, showing the multiplicity of jobs.

Most of these persons devote only a fourth or a fifth of their time to this work. If they are not regular members of the staff, they are music teachers, clubwomen, artists, art teachers, or in some other occupation full time and doing this critical writing on the side. When the author was editing the book page and the art-drama-music page of a small daily, he also was city editor of the paper—a typical situation.

Characteristic of the two main ways to obtain critical writing for a newspaper is the practice of the Syracuse (N. Y.) *Post-Standard,* a morning daily of more than 100,000 circulation. Miss Nevart Apikian, of the general reporting staff, criticizes the new movies as they arrive, but she also puts the church page together for Saturday and covers a variety of city events as well. Dr. William Fleming, chairman of the Fine Arts Concentration in the College of Liberal Arts at Syracuse University, a pianist and teacher of music, and author of books on music and the other arts, writes the criticisms of major musical events. He goes to the *Post-Standard's* city room only to write his reviews and hand them to the city desk.

American dailies, then, employ possibly a few hundred full-time writers on the arts. These write principally in the big cities where there is enough work to keep them busy (the New York *Times Book Review* alone, as explained in another chapter, has a staff of full-time critics as large as the *Post-Standard's* whole editorial department). The rest, in our tabulation, are like Dr. Fleming in their relationship to the publication.

Weekly newspapers, although there are many more of them (approximately 9,000 weeklies to 1,800 dailies of general circulation), employ no full-time critics whatsoever, and depend upon specialists, volunteers, or ambitious staff members. The typical weekly contains little or no critical writing on any of the arts. What appears is an occasional reportorial piece by a staff member when some performer appears in the community; or a criticism by a local person who volunteers the work for the sake of the art, self-expression, or prestige; or critical writing that is included with syndicated material such as prepared editorials, comic strips, feature articles, and other copy it is difficult for the weekly to produce.

Although they outnumber newspapers in the United States by several hundred, magazines generally do not give comparable space to criticism because the bulk of them are highly specialized. Of the 8,000 house publications (also called industrial publications or house organs) issued by individual industries, businesses, and other groups, the majority are magazines. But only in a few externals (which are for consumers or the general public) does critical writing appear, for most house publications are internals and intended for employees and are much like country weeklies in their content.

A little critical writing appears in the approximately 2,000 trade and technical publications, usually lumped together as business publications. This writing is almost entirely about books related to the magazine's subject matter (the ice-cream industry, the furniture business, swimming pool sales and the like).

The two remaining major groups—the general consumer and the nontechnical specialized magazines—carry the weight of criticism in American periodicals.

All magazines for each of the arts contain critical writing. So do the periodicals that appeal especially to people of broad intellectual interests. A smaller quantity of evaluation has its place, also, in the women's, shelter, and family magazines and even in periodicals of fashion and homemaking. Hundreds that deal with religion print book reviews regularly; even the most specialized magazine of the sciences makes room for reviews of new books and the radio and television programs of its area. Moreover, thousands of full-length critical articles appear annually in these magazines.

The Space for Criticism

Another gauge of the extent of criticism in journalism is the amount of space devoted to it. Here, again, the vastness of this country's journalism makes accurate measurement a stupendous task which no part of the industry has either seen fit or been able to make. A clue to the amount of space allotted to criticism of the arts is the amount of advertising of those arts. But an analysis of a *Newspaper Rates and Data* report by Standard Rate and Data, Inc., a firm that gathers information about advertising appearing in various media, shows that any figure advanced from this sole available clue would be highly unreliable. Scores of dailies that have regular book, radio-television, and other pages of coverage and criticism did not report them.[2] Only by examining at least seven issues of every newspaper or by making an expensive national survey would it be possible to report a reasonably close figure. While such special pages are not as numerous, evidently, as those for food and sports, they run into the hundreds. A sampling reveals that generally they allot space for critical writing.

The relative place of the various media, in respect to their criticism of the arts, might be indicated by this list of the media and the arts they criticize.

	Books	Maga-zines	Motion Pictures	News-papers	Radio	Syndi-cates*	Tele-vision
Architecture	x	x	0	0	0	0	0
Dancing	x	x	0	x	0	x	0
Drama	x	x	0	x	0	x	0
Literature	x	x	0	x	x	x	x
Motion pictures	x	x	0	x	0	x	0
Music	x	x	0	x	0	x	0
Painting	x	x	0	x	0	x	0
Photography	x	x	0	x	0	x	0
Radio-television	x	x	0	x	0	x	0
Recordings	x	x	0	x	0	x	0
Sculpture	x	x	0	x	0	x	0

x = criticism is offered by the medium.
0 = criticism is not offered or only rarely.
* This includes the wire services.

[2] This may be explained by: (a) the form used to gather the information was not filled in completely; (b) many newspapers have Sunday special sections and noted only this fact without indicating what is covered by these sections; and (c) rates are given for book, theater, and other such subjects without indicating that these advertisements are or are not on special pages.

The above list was prepared from the point of view of a person who wants a regular source of criticism of one or more of the arts. It is clear that it is the printed media to which such a person must turn; similarly, to them writers and professional journalists must look for outlets for their work. Books, while slower in publication and only once in frequency of issue, print criticism of all the arts. Magazines provide more, and more rapidly than books, but their offerings may not be of as high or of as lasting quality. Newspapers and syndicates do almost as well but are somewhat narrower in scope and shallower than books or magazines as media. Except for a rare documentary, the motion picture offers no criticism of the arts, including itself, and radio and television do a little of it only in book-review or general-arts programs or in an occasional panel discussion. It should be noted, also, that neither of these electronic media attempts any self-criticism through its own medium. This failure may spring partly from unwillingness, but it also is logically based on the belief that the mass public which views and listens is not interested in media evaluation.

The "Eastern Monopoly"

And is it true that the best criticism comes largely from a half-dozen so-called Eastern centers of culture? It is true that the publishing industry is centered in the northeastern United States. The large Atlantic seaboard cities from Washington to Boston, and the small towns near them which increasingly are the addresses of periodical and book publishers (because of lower rentals and property values) do contain a concentration of this industry.

But it also is a fact that numerous small-circulation magazines of the arts are issued from many other parts of the country (*see* Chapter 12), particularly university communities. These periodicals contain some of the most perceptive criticism of the fine and popular arts available in journalism. The American newspaper, it also must be remembered, is not centralized in source as are books and magazines. No one paper serves the whole nation, for the country is physically too large. Newspaper critics of the arts are dispersed, then, and while mere dispersal does not mean quality, it would be a prejudiced statement if one declared that the only competent critics are in a few big-city offices. The quality of their work differs by the arts they criticize, to be sure. But the fact is that no one sees the entire American critical picture scientifically. It might be possible in some tiny nation with only a few dozen publications to read every line of critical writing produced in a given period and arrive at a conclusion about its amount, depth, and other characteristics. But this cannot be done in a land which produces such a stupendous amount of printed matter as does the United States.

In the preparation of this book the author read literally thousands of pieces of critical writing, from large and small publications, by renowned and unknown critics alike. From this, as well as from many years of reading criticism and from listening to oral criticism, he concludes that there is meritorious critical writing west of Albany to the Pacific, and south of Washington to the West Indies, and that it is about time it be appreciated outside its regional limits.

The extent of criticism in the American journalistic scene, then, is more important than is commonly realized. No one knows how many persons, for gain or as a labor of love or for prestige or self-expression or some other intangible reward, are engaged in it.

The Functions

The place that critical writing has achieved in the American journalistic media to some extent helps determine its functions. That place, as we have seen, is not known precisely. But it is substantial, in personnel and space, especially in the printed media.

The functions of critical writing coincide with those of all journalistic writing. The principal purposes of journalism are to inform, influence, and entertain. Critical writing does all of these, but it emphasizes the function of influence. It is a brother to the editorial (including the signed opinion column), but only a cousin of the news story, the feature, and the article. No relative at all is it of the poem, short story, or other fiction. Critical are few such metropolises. More space is devoted to certain of the arts seasonally because of the greater possibilities of advertising—summer theaters, for example. Another function, then, is to earn money directly for the medium. This, too, may stultify honest criticism.

Finally, critical writing sometimes is published to obtain prestige. It can indeed provide it. But publishers (or program makers) who present it for this purpose chiefly are not necessarily lovers of the arts, but only wish their publications or programs to be in good company, to be seen in the right places. Sometimes what begins from this motive grows into genuine interest. So long as the rest of the publication earns sufficient revenue, the luxury of prestige-getting is continued; if interest on the part of readers is developed, it may persist even in hard times.

Publishers of critical writing on the arts find in one or more of these functions their justification. It is interesting, then, to speculate on what determines the amount of reading matter or time allotted to the various artistic divisions. It appears to be decided in this way: if there is sufficient advertising (or sponsorship) for a special section or program, that amount will be assigned. More or less appears to depend upon an estimate of what the public wants (except for the increasingly rare individualistic editor, publisher, or owner who insists on some given amount of attention because of his personal desires in the matter, as John C. Shaffer, the publisher, saw to it that the Chicago *Evening Post* issued a special supplement for books and another for arts every week). Using reader-interest surveys, letters, and what they consider their knowledge of the cultural level of the United States public, publishers of most newspapers and magazines years ago concluded that the public is overwhelmingly interested in sports, but scarcely at all, by comparison, in any of the arts, except those debated ones called radio, television, photography, records, and cinema. Many of them have attempted to defy these evidences of indifference, but most have concluded that, in a day of sky-high materials and labor costs, allotting increased space to the arts cannot be attempted successfully. Radio and television make virtually no attempt to criticize the arts in

writing emphasizes opinion; news writing emphasizes
tion; the feature stresses human interest; the article
emphasis on background or explanation. Any capabl
review or criticism also conveys information and, if it
well written, offers even a measure of entertainment;
a humorous piece of criticism is fun to read.

In fulfilling its function of influencing readers, criti
serves as a guide. When a reader picks up a newspaper
zine to read a movie or book criticism, for instance (o
the trouble to hear someone review a book or play or
expects several things. He wants to know what the book
(information). He also wants to be told what the review
of the book (influence or opinion). He wants to learn if it
his time to read it (guidance). He hopes, as well, to e
writing of the review itself (entertainment).

But there are other functions that criticism in Americ
nalism must perform. It must promote. Critics may not lik
sensitive readers are sometimes disgusted with promoti
guised as criticism. This promotional function has reach
magnitude that it has become an evil of the critical pro
To many a publisher, theater director, or broadcast p
manager criticism is primarily a publicity tool, a factor in d
ing a favorable public attitude toward the work of art in qu
Here it is that art in America has had a tie with commer
has been a source of trouble to critics for a half century.

Criticism is regarded by some entrepreneurs of the ar
as a means of attracting advertising accounts. It certainly i
a means, although its effectiveness as such varies accord
the art form, the type of publication, and the community
side New York City's *Herald Tribune* and *Times,* a sprit
of other big-city dailies, and such magazines as *Harper's
Atlantic,* and *The Saturday Review,* for instance, book-adver
revenue is not great enough to convince any publisher th
should run a book page purely for the financial returns. R
television, and motion-picture advertising, on the other har
an important part of any daily paper's income. In cities
many legitimate theaters a drama page pays for itself, but t

view of the number of artistic programs that have failed to hold audiences.

The impact of these several functions upon criticism itself is strong. A journalist who is given to understand that his writing should inform, influence, guide, and entertain readers, as well as promote the art itself so that it attracts advertising to the publication and lends prestige to the magazine or paper, must be a superjournalist to succeed. It takes a bold critic, indeed, to damn a performance when he knows that the same page will carry a splendiferous advertisement for that same book, play, or concert. The purely journalistic task of informing, influencing, and the like becomes immensely difficult, for in discharging it honestly he may ruin advertising accounts, as witness the long history of quarrels between the Schuberts and other theatrical entrepreneurs on the one hand and the press on the other.

An equally real problem created by the diverse functions of criticism is the necessity to perform all these functions when the work under criticism is that of a foe or a friend. Here the danger is not only of offending an advertiser but also of offending a friend or seeming to play favorites. Not all of this is intentional; likely as not it is the result of blind spots developed by the critic. Many a literary critic is a friendly fellow who encourages an author to complete a book; when the volume is sent to him for review, he rolls the log as expertly as a Canadian woodsman. If he is a critic of good taste his judgment probably is correct, but it appears to be suspect. History, on the other hand, is full of accounts of authors or artists and critics who could not get along with each other and carried on enmities lasting decades.

The straight news reporter or even the feature writer has a proper defense. He can say truthfully: "That is the way it happened. Those are the facts; you cannot blame me for life as it is." But the critic draws upon himself as a source; it is what *he* thinks, and the damnation is upon him for sheltering such opinions. This is the risk of remaining in one of the few areas of journalism not yet beset by pattern or formula writing. The privilege may be worth the risk.

Critics' Views of Functions

Practical critics are aware, of course, of all these pragmatic considerations. Only the aesthetic critic, absorbed in the philosophies of criticism and as unconcerned with the outer world as is the pure scientist, ignores the impact of commerce on criticism.

Literary journalists have explained what they consider to be the functions of criticism. Anthony West, novelist and critic whose reviews have appeared often in *The New Yorker,* when defending himself from an attack by Granville Hicks in *The New Leader* in 1956, wrote in *The Saturday Review* his explanation of the function of criticism and reviewing. He said:

"For me, at any rate, criticism and reviewing are a part of the great debate which keeps society alive: books express ideas and reviewers and critics are legitimately occupied in discussing the ideas they express."

On the other hand, we have the views of Oscar Thompson, music critic for the New York *Evening Post* from 1928 to 1935, one of the editors of *Musical America,* and teacher of a course in musical criticism. He said in *Practical Musical Criticism,* the one book devoted wholly to such criticism, that criticism "has one clear function, so central and dominating that all others may be regarded as subsidiary or supplementary." It ". . . is to hold up a mirror to what has been composed or performed and to the performance."

This function is essentially the reporting or informational one already discussed. From there he went on to value judgments, for he said: "Its purpose is to present a clear picture of what the music is, with its good points and bad. . . ."

We soon find that critics, like publishers, programmers, and the public, are not in agreement as to what the exact functions of criticism are or should be.

The Criticisms of
Journalistic Criticism

J. Donald Adams of the New York *Times Book Review* has called criticism "a monkish practice, divorced from life, bastardized by the assumption of scientific method, written in intolerable English, a jargonized medium of exchange between a group of individuals talking to one another and busily thumbing their noses at the average intelligent reader."

Granville Hicks, book columnist for both *The New Leader* and *The Saturday Review* during the late 1950's, declared in 1956 that "although there are hundreds of newspapers and magazines in which books are reviewed, there are probably not more than twenty that try to maintain even moderately high standards of literary journalism." This was preliminary to a long attack on book criticism in *The New Yorker,* and by Anthony West in particular.

Then we have the words of Ralph Thompson, while chief reader for the Book-of-the-Month Club, uttered in the same year for the *Bulletin* of the American Society of Newspaper Editors. His was a scorching commentary on newspaper book reviewing in America that has hardly been equaled: "There are probably more lame, careless, lazy or pussyfooting book reviews printed in American newspapers in the course of an average month than there are hairs on the average author's head," he began. He went on to describe the situation as "a scandal."

These criticisms of journalistic criticism are by no means confined to book reviewing. Theodore L. Shaw has filled most of a book, *Precious Rubbish*, with quotations which he uses to expose critics of the various arts as guilty of producing an "appalling barrage of ritzy twaddle." Such attacks have been leveled at critics of painting and sculpture, television, music, and the drama with similar bitterness.

Nor are such attacks new. Since the occupation of critic persists, newcomers to the critical world should not be discouraged by them, but try, instead, to learn from them. Brooks Atkinson, Walter Kerr, Edmund Wilson, and scores of others have gone on despite denunciations of their breed that can be traced back many years.

Frank Luther Mott, the historian of American journalism, discovered that as far back as 1835 literary criticism was damned. In a widely quoted lecture by Edward S. Gould, it was denounced for its superficiality, fondness for generalization instead of analysis, hyperbole, and generous extracts rather than discussion. At the same time, Edgar Allan Poe accused magazines of using indiscriminate praise in their reviews. Arthur Waugh, writing in *The Critic* in 1896, lamented that "In all the wilderness of reviewing, how seldom do we encounter a real review!" And the very next year Norman Hapgood, a foremost American journalist, declared in *The Bookman* that "In no country is the current comment on books more lacking in thought and workmanship. . . . In comment on the drama the same low level is unbroken."

These are only a few of the many imprecations against criticism and critics in this nation's history. They come from widely known as well as obscure persons; some denouncers are themselves critics.

Praise as Well

But it is not a one-sided story. There has been praise, as well, especially in more recent years.

C. P. Snow, British novelist and businessman, told Maurice Dolbier of the New York *Herald Tribune Books* that "Your American reviewing differs from ours in that you're more interested in what is in the books than in how what is in the books is said. You're more like the Russians in that you know . . . I think it's a good thing. Pure estheticism is no more healthy in reviewing than it is in fiction writing. . . ."

From a widely respected American source, we have what Malcolm Cowley said in 1954 in his book, *The Literary Situation*. It was that "critics are in fashion today. One hears it maintained that this is an age of criticism in the special sense that the Elizabethan period was the age of the poetic drama and the Victorian period the age of the novel . . . The best of it appears in books with a limited sale and magazines with a small body of readers. But the critics today have power and status; there are more of them than ever before, including more writers of original talent, and they are listened to with greater attention, because they speak with more authority than most of the novelists or poets."

This statement is followed by an assertion that writing in the critical field is growing in quantity and is generally of higher quality. "Reviews of current books—to start with a humble corner of the field—are better written and better informed than they were thirty years ago," Mr. Cowley goes on to say. "Too many of them used to be dashed off by boys just out of college . . . Now the reviewers are much older on the average, they are paid at somewhat higher rates, and they seem to feel that they will be additionally rewarded for brilliant work: that they will be admired by their friends and will earn better positions in the literary, publishing, or academic worlds. Accordingly they express themselves with care and their reviews have acquired a professional quality, in a field that used to be pre-empted by amateurs."

And there is more, from other sources. But, as usual, it is easier to find denunciation than approval, for the former takes less effort to write.

Below the Generalizations

If critics are to learn from those who criticize them, they cannot be content merely with scanning either the compliments or the brickbats. They need to examine specifically what is below the generalizations. What, in general then, are the specific areas of weakness in journalistic criticism singled out by its critics? A study of the attacks reveals several.

1. *Too many critical writers lack qualification for the job.*

Joseph Conrad, in a letter to Alfred A. Knopf in 1913, which Mr. Knopf quotes in a 1958 *Atlantic Monthly* article, put it temperately when he said, "And you cannot deny that the majority of writers of notices in newspapers are men of average tastes."

Pliny quoted Zeuxis, who wrote about 2,300 years ago, as saying that "Criticism comes easier than craftsmanship."

Probably the most amusing exposition of this viewpoint is the tale told by Theodore H. Parker, a long-time critical writer for the Hartford (Conn.) *Courant*. In *The American Editor* he related in 1957 that he once knew an art critic who was color-blind. This journalist, aptly designated by Mr. Parker as a "dichromatic reporter," managed to hold his job as long as his wife, who had normal vision, accompanied him to the art exhibits. This incident leads to the not unlikely suspicion of the existence of tone-deaf music critics, art critics with mirror-vision, myopic television reviewers, and hypermetropic drama critics.

Ralph Thompson, of the Book-of-the-Month Club, part of whose blast at reviewers already has been noted, also said that "One curse of newspaper review departments everywhere is the office boy with nothing to do for the next couple of hours. Another is the local clubwoman whose children are now grown but who still adores Thomas Hardy. Among the others is the girl graduate who did a thesis on William Faulkner last June, the novelist who is stuck on the third chapter of his first novel, and the expansive city-room type who recently bought a new house and still has a couple of bookshelves to fill."

We come still closer to evidence from an assertion by Herschel Brickell, a widely experienced reviewer, author, editor, and anthologist, who said in a chapter of a book which he edited (*Writers on Writing*) that "Most book reviewing in the United States of America at this moment is honest and not very competent. It is honest because we are, in general, blessed with an honest press, but the trouble is that few newspapers or magazines feel they can afford to pay very much, if anything, for book reviewing, and this explains the generally low level of competence."

As one examines the careers of many critics, it is difficult to deny that these charges often are merited. We may not have many dichromatic or tone-deaf critics, but a wide reading of journalistic criticism justifies these conclusions:

Most of the critics of the various arts whose work appears in the 11,000 daily and weekly newspapers of general circulation have not had adequate preparation in either the arts they criticize or the art of criticism itself. More are capable, however, than generally is realized. It is one of the aims of this book to show this to be true and to help improve the grade of journalistic criticism by indicating how others become adequately qualified.

Relatively little criticism appears in the 12,500 magazines of various frequencies of issues in the United States, since the bulk of these serve specialties. The criticism that does appear, by and large, in magazines of the various arts and periodicals seriously concerned with public affairs and ideas is of a generally high order and the critics are qualified for their tasks.

In the next two chapters the reader will find a fuller discussion of the qualifications that the aspiring critic must attempt to acquire.

2. *Too often critics are unfair or biased.*

This accusation was dramatized in 1958 when Steve Allen, television comedian, poet, and short-story writer, wrote an attack on Jack O'Brian, television critic of the New York *Journal-American*. This appeared in *The Village Voice*, a Greenwich Village tabloid weekly that is generous with space for the arts, at about the time that Hy Gardner, syndicated columnist for the New York *Herald Tribune* and also a television performer, suggested that advertising agencies remove ads from newspapers guilty of "unfair television criticism."

Allen's blast, which filled ten columns in two issues of *The Village Voice*, included such charges as: "Mr. O'Brian has assumed the role of the neighborhood bully. . . . He is derelict in his duty to his readers, unethical in his methods, and beneath the respect of the industry because his column is frequently an outlet for his personal emotional delinquencies rather than a reflection of intelligent, fair, responsible criticism." O'Brian gave the whole controversy little attention, but it aroused discussion of the nature of television criticism in the press.

Gardner's views received more serious discussion than Allen's, because they contained the seeds of censorship. He told *Advertising Age,* after the speech before the League of Advertising Agencies in which he originally had made his proposal, that: "If I had a show which was being lambasted with great glee and regularity by a newspaper's television critic, serving no constructive purpose other than building up the by-liner's ego and readership, I'd yank my ads for that show out of that paper quicker than you can drop an option."

Gardner added that he had seen many sponsors wasting money by buying space to ask viewers to watch the same program that a television column beside the advertisement "rips to ribbons again and again and again." He said that he'd "swallow the criticism, accept it and be grateful for it if it is constructive—but if the needling was constant and malicious I'd be damned if I'd support that kind of damaging doggerel with my dollars." He also said that many critics came from other assignments on their papers and are not qualified by either background or experience for their jobs.

Such complaints, with less drastic remedies suggested for them, have been heard for scores of years about critics of all the arts. Spyros Skouras, motion-picture magnate, for example, has complained that the motion-picture critics are too harsh about the movies. "They're not fair to us," he told Art Buchwald, syndicated columnist. "I don't think the American motion-picture business has been courageous enough. The critics should be conscious of the fact we are fighting for our lives [this was in 1958] and they should not put nails in our coffins. The funny thing is the pictures the critics criticize are the ones the public wants to see. The ones they praise, in the majority, are the flops.

"I love critics. I never complain about the review of one picture. It's their attitude toward pictures that I don't like. They don't see it from the public's viewpoint. Besides, they never stop at being critics. They become writers, directors, and producers. I think they're incompetent to pass judgment on films."

3. *Critics sometimes have a distorted sense of values.*

This alleged distortion has been typically complained about by Edward L. Bernays, a leading public relations expert and author of numerous books on this occupation. Writing to *Publishers' Weekly* he said that readers are baffled by the conflicting opinions of critics but "even more baffled by differences in value placed on books." He cited as an example the fact that Simone de Beauvoir's *The Second Sex* received a paragraph review in *Newsweek* but six and a half pages in *The Saturday Review*. The newsmagazine had called it "a singular mixture of pedantry, nonsense, quotations from novels, case histories, and psychological, anthropological, and other works, beginning with Satre and ending with Marx." *The Saturday Review* carried evaluations of it by six different eminent critics.

One of the most telling complaints of this sort was written by John Steinbeck. His letter in *The Saturday Review* of February 27, 1954, appeared just before publication of his novel, *East of Eden.*

"I'm too old to go through publication labor again, to wait for the reviews, to have my heart broken, to read the considered words of critics (considered for two hours) on work that has taken me four years to write and fifty years to live. Once I read and wept over reviews. I wondered what the LORDS GOD would have the graciousness to say about my pulings. And then one time I put the criticisms all together and I found that they canceled each other out and left me non-existent." The stage set, Steinbeck added:

"I'm tired now. I wonder whether I can go through the reviews again. I know them in advance. The *New Yorker*, which will never forgive me for not being Proust. God! if I could only write in French and have a bad translation I would get a good review there. Monastic *Time* will turn out the pin-striped monks who will intone, 'IT IS A GOOD BOOK BUT IT FAILS'. . . . *The Chicago Tribune* will have confused me with England to

my benefit and the Hearst papers will spell my name Steinberg
and review my latest volume of cartoons. And last—the intense
young men with receding hairlines who are too smart to do a
daily Piece—they save (I think they call them interpretations)
for a book. They will find me *passé* and will reveal the source
of my material. It usually turns out to be a French Trappist of
the eighteenth century. I always have to look him up with the
book in my hand because I not only never heard of him but
can't spell him if I get too far in the book. No! I'm too goddamn
old for it. There was a time when Clifton Fadiman and I were
young. He was the book section of the Heinz Pickle works and
the dew was fresh on my damask page. But now I am an elder
statesman and he has gone on to bigger things with Lucky
Strikes. I wonder, as he delivers a *mot* and a carton to a tap
dancer, whether he will remember that he once said I had
promise. That was before he denounced me as a traitor to my
nation when I wrote *The Moon Is Down*. I never blamed him
for that. He was between products."

Bernard Kalb, then of *The Saturday Review* staff, commented:
"Steinbeck, it turned out once the reviews actually appeared,
hadn't done a bad job at all in calling the critical shots. *The
New Yorker* panned it, as predicted. *Time* said yes and no, mostly
no, as predicted. *The Chicago Trib* was neither hot nor cold. A
Hearst newspaper review wasn't exactly bowled over, as predicted. As for Fadiman ('We're both good friends again,' Steinbeck said the other day. 'We're both older and softer'), he turned
out to be pretty much on Steinbeck's side, though he did find
a couple of things in the novel he didn't care for. Regardless,
East of Eden wound up on the best-seller lists shortly after it
came out, to remain there for weeks and weeks and weeks."

4. *Criticism is not creative.*

S. R. Littlewood tells a story in his book, *The Art of Dramatic
Criticism*, of a farce called *When Knights Were Bold*, being
shown in England. It did not go well at its first performance. He
was in the dressing room of James Welch, one of the actors,
who was much upset at the way things were going.

"He put this down to the apathetic demeanour of the critics

present," Mr. Littlewood wrote. " 'I know those —— critics,' he said, shaking his fist in the direction of the auditorium, 'disappointed dramatists, every man jack of them!' "

Such an accusation is part of the more general one heard ever since there have been critics: that criticism is not creative. It has been likened to a parasite on "truly" creative work, such as poetry, plays, novels, music, and the other arts. To this attitude George Jean Nathan has a reply which is consoling defense of criticism as creative writing. In his *Testament of a Critic* he said he objected to the contention that "the phrase 'creative writing' must be reserved for novelists, poets and writers of a kind, however bad, and that it cannot truthfully be visited upon others, however good. Criticism, according to the definition, does not come under the head of creation and, as a consequence, such things as Dryden's 'Essay of Dramatic Poesy' are not creative writing whereas such things as Zane Grey's novels presumably are . . . Frank Harris' journalism has often been creative writing of a high order. So has Shaw's and Wells'. What, too, of Addison's, Steele's, Swift's, and Lamb's? And as for critical creative writing, what of Philip Sidney's, Corneille's, Samuel Johnson's, Lessing's, Voltaire's, Schiller's, and Zola's?"

5. *The critic's politics must be right.*

A reader of *The New Republic* wrote: "If you replaced Gerald Johnson with David Lawrence and signed up Walter Kerr as your drama critic, *The New Republic* would be a more appropriate magazine for the art criticism of Frank Getlein."

To which the editors answered thus:

"Art criticism is, of course, Mr. Getlein's province: the relation of art and politics is a common concern. And here, all epithets about 'objective' and 'nonobjective' art aside, our subscriber raises a familiar argument that we have never been able fully to comprehend.

"To be a true liberal, implies this subscriber, one must also be for abstract expression in painting. Why? Because abstract expression is contemporary? So is the hydrogen bomb. Because it is exploring the hitherto unexplored? So is Dr. J. B. Rhine . . . Are we delinquent in not endorsing all his works as well? If liberals in politics are necessarily abstract expressionists in art, does it follow that abstract expressionists must necessarily be liberals? We hope not. Will some kind reader guide us out of the tunnel?"

No reader came forth to do so. It is popular for discussion groups and writers of letters to the "idea" magazines to worry about this problem. Few editors of the magazines and papers of current problems take the view of *The New Republic*, however. The conservative journals (*National Review*, for instance) will not tolerate a writer usually identified with liberal or radical publications (by which might be meant *The Nation*, *The Commonweal*, *The Progressive* and others in that group). These latter, while they will publish an occasional critical piece by an ultraconservative (that is, one who feels more at home on the editorial pages of *The Saturday Evening Post* than on those of *The New Leader*) similarly would not publish regularly the critical writings of such a conservative, whether his conservatism be in the arts or in politics.

6. *Journalistic critics are no more than promoters.*

We have already discussed the relationship between commerce and criticism, the dangers of logrolling, and the ease with which the critic can be trapped into showing favoritism. There is still another angle which is a source of complaint. Morton Dauwen Zabel, editor of *Literary Opinion in America*, expressed it this way:

"The loss of literary journalists and reviewers entails less regret. A number of these have written valuable propaganda for modern books and writers; a few, like H. L. Mencken, have prepared the day for remarkable gains in creative writing itself; others have done work in the Americanization of the literary viewpoint. . . . But for the most part this activity has nothing to do with criticism. It is an adjunct of the book-trade, of high-pressure literary promotion, of book-clubs, advertising, and the business of exploitation that has gradually deprived the country of its few reputable literary monthlies and reviews [this was published in 1937]. To such service many lively writers have surrendered their talents. . . ."

7. *The quality of critical writing is low.*

In selecting expressions of the criticisms of criticism the author has had to confine himself to a few passages only. A typical statement on the quality of critical writing was made by Vivienne Koch, writing in the spring, 1957, *Partisan Review*, which is concerned with television. Possibly because it is one of the newest of the popular arts and therefore more vulnerable, being unformed, or because television programs are in general of low caliber and critics who fail to attack its weaknesses are considered deficient, this medium has won many slaps.

"The whole issue, incidentally, of a serious, responsible and pragmatic television criticism," Miss Koch wrote, "has yet to be thought out at even the most rudimentary level. What passes for television criticism at the moment ranges from the flip, gossipy opinions of John Crosby . . . to the hortatory, semi-editorial pronouncements of Jack Gould . . . , but it is badly written and utterly rudderless in terms of aesthetic moorings, either in the way of background and taste, or in the way of empirically derived values of the *possible* in this medium. There is, at quite a different level of engagement, the thoughtful if somewhat old-fashioned writing of Gilbert Seldes in a book like *The Public Arts*. Unfortunately, however, in his weekly television columns in *The Saturday Review* Seldes is given over to a generalizing habit rather than to the grubby work of ad hoc discriminations which television so sorely wants."

These accusations—and the author's files are filled with others like them on any of the arts—are not recorded here preliminary to a reply. Analysis and adequate rebuttal in themselves would comprise another book; furthermore, there is no rebuttal possible, in the author's opinion, on some of the attacks: they are entirely justified. They are noted only as a reminder to critics that if they think the complaints valid they must follow methods and practices that will not lay them open to these charges.

It is obvious that with so many thousands of persons writing critically about the arts some unfairness, bad English, uninformed opinions, and distortions of values will result. The author refuses to generalize about these criticisms beyond the few already listed. No one knows what *all* critics write on any one of the arts, much less on every one of them. In any case, it is a healthier situation to maintain conditions that permit any view to be expressed, whether competent or incompetent, even though artists sometimes are hurt in the process. What is the alternative? To do as in totalitarian lands of both the left and the right: to enforce uniformity.

In the author's view, the bulk of American journalistic critical writing is better than the mass of women's page writing, sports writing, and local reporting. This is not to say, however, that the critics should be content with their present achievements.

As an Occupation

> *MAN, 51, M. Ed., B. A. Psych., disgusted with it all,*
> *but eclectically admiring Brameld, Fromm, Montagu,*
> *Lindner, other rebels, desires job writing criticism, appre-*
> *ciations. Samples ready. Box F-267.*
> *—The Saturday Review*

Some people have the idea that the temperament of the critic should be like that of the man who placed the above classified advertisement. They also believe that it is so much of a full-fledged occupation that one can obtain a job in it merely by advertising.

What Arnold Bennett the novelist said about English book reviewing in the very first year of the century is still essentially true about American journalistic criticism in general.

"To enter this field," he wrote in *The Truth About an Author*, ". . . with the intention of tilling it to a profitable fiscal harvest is an enterprise in the nature of a forlorn hope."

T. S. Eliot echoed this opinion more than half a century later when he said that ". . . serious literary journalism is an inadequate as well as a precarious means of support for all but a very few. . . ."

The practicing critic who reads this book knows that, with some drawbacks, critical writing for journalism has many attractions as an occupation, but that big money is not one of them. Certain writers who have regular columns or other fixed space, and a somewhat larger number who combine critical writing with editing do well. But critical writing, whether of reviews and criticisms or of the critical article, is much like free-lance writing in that few of its practitioners have to pay a big income tax.

The would-be critic, therefore, might as well face facts and reconcile himself to them. They have not discouraged thousands of free lancers of other types of journalism. Nor do the editors of the art, literary and other journals lack applicants for posts as critics, although they say the quality could be higher. Books

---

THE FOURTH ESTATE . . .   By Trent

"I cover movies in the afternoon, music and legit shows at night and late floor shows after that."

Courtesy, *Editor & Publisher*

of critical writing come steadily from the presses. Not much of this work is done, however, by people who are critics only.

Stanley Meisler, a Washington newspaperman, describing in the spring, 1958, *Journalism Quarterly* a study he made of the work of entertainment editors on newspapers in large cities outside New York, began his report by saying:

"The entertainment editor of a large metropolitan daily works in so special a field only students too foolish or confident or romantic to be deterred by reality can set out for the job. Even if they dare, students have little to go on. Where do entertainment editors come from? How do they get their jobs? What do they do?"

Much of what he discovered applies to all the non-New York full-timers who do critical work along with their regular journalism, whether it be of music, drama, television, or any of the other arts. Mr. Meisler can say nothing effectively to discourage the really dedicated young man or woman who will be a critic or bust. Many of these there have been in even more discouraging times than at mid-century, as this chapter tries to show. The reincarnations of the Burton Rascoes, Ward Morehouses, and many others may be momentarily disheartened by Mr. Meisler's findings and even by the conservativeness of this chapter, but once they realize that, although critical writing as an occupation economically amounts to little, it offers many other rewards, they will go on trying to become critics.

The revelation by Mr. Meisler that most of these editors did not expect entertainment writers to have special training is examined more closely in the next chapter, where that topic belongs. We can pass on to his point that a critic, reviewer, or editor of critical writing values his prestige highly; this is one of the non-monetary rewards. He likes his by-lines and the fact that "some of the more cultured people in the community know his name. He envisions himself as a vital member of the community." After indicating other findings, which are dealt with elsewhere in this book, Mr. Meisler concludes from his study that critical writing "is a job journalists, moving through the regular channel of a newspaper, hold fast once they get it."

Chapter 2 of this book has tried to indicate the place of critical writing in American mass communication. This place—small but growing as the cultural explosion continues—reveals something of the nature of the occupation. Critics often as not must be reporters, desk editors, news editors, departmental editors. The job is limited in reaching aesthetic heights by the educational level of the readers and listeners. As a job, criticism in journalism divides neatly into two sections. One is made up of salaried persons, employed by a publication, and giving all or part of their working time to critical writing. The other consists of those persons who do not depend upon a publication for their main stipend. They are teachers, performers of the arts, businessmen with an artistic flair, or, as we have seen earlier, newsmen or magazinists or broadcasters whose main income is derived from serving journalism some other way.

Those to whom criticism is a full-time job are the rarae aves, the elite of the occupation. Possibly the most widely known of these rare birds is J. Brooks Atkinson, drama critic of the New York *Times,* whose extraordinary place in the world of journalistic criticism was dramatized in 1958 when more than one hundred playwrights, directors, song writers, actors, producers, and labor union officials honored him. Oscar Hammerstein II was master of ceremonies, Mary Martin sang to accompaniment by Richard Rodgers, and the critic was given a silver tray and asked to make a speech. In the course of the evening a letter from Moss Hart was read. "Whoever heard of theatre-folk," it read, "giving a party for a dramatic critic? A critic on a spit, turning slowly over hot coals, is the usual fantasy." Ralph Bellamy, Helen Hayes, and many other theater notables bowed to Atkinson.

Justin Brooks Atkinson began to write drama criticism early, although he had no special preparation for it. Enthusiastic about the journalistic life from his boyhood in Massachusetts, he was a district reporter for the Springfield *Daily News* after he left Harvard with a B. A. degree. In 1919, at 25, after military service and a brief time as an English instructor at Dartmouth, he covered police for the Boston *Evening Transcript.* Then he got the opportunity to assist Harold Taylor Parker, noted drama critic who signed his reviews only with his initials and made them a power in New England. Three years later Atkinson became editor of the New York *Times'* Sunday book section. In another three he returned to play criticism when Stark Young resigned from the *Times.* Except for a stint as war correspondent in 1942 (which he did with distinction), Atkinson has held his prized top spot in criticism ever since. For the surprise party at Sardi's, March 2, 1958, a special edition of the *Times'* Sunday drama page was prepared, entirely devoted to him, and in the usual type-dress of that widely read section.

Lewis Funke, writing in the *Times'* house organ, *Times Talk,* punningly described the life of the drama critic as actually all work and no play. He pictured some of the extracurricular duties: balancing a monkey on one shoulder and a parrot on another while trying to interview Tallulah Bankhead, who at one time had a virtual menagerie with her when she traveled. Or holding a star's baby while its mother prepares the formula during an interview.

Funke, himself a member of the drama staff, explains that the drama writer has more to do than sit comfortably at about 150 first nights during the regular season. He notes the need to correlate the schedules of around 150 summer theaters, keeping track of the regular season statistics, reading what other newspapers and the magazines say about the theater, attending luncheons and dinners for trade purposes, and dealing with the hypersensitive people who comprise the stage world.

Brooks Atkinson takes care of most of the reviews and also writes special critical articles for the Sunday section, with seven other drama department staffers doing critical writing as well as the other tasks. Criticism and reporting of drama news are thoroughly intertwined; Atkinson is the only one of the eight who does reviewing almost exclusively, but he also appears at social and professional functions.

Compare this life with that of a typical part-time critic who is a full-time member of her newspaper's staff: Miss Nevart Apikian, movie reviewer for the Syracuse (N. Y.) *Post-Standard,* mentioned briefly in an earlier chapter. Miss Apikian, a university journalism school graduate, divides her time between reviewing all important new movies, preparing the Saturday church page, covering such city-desk assignments as food and fashion shows, and handling stories over the telephone when her help is needed in the city room.

Miss Apikian also had no special preparation for criticism of the art she is interested in. Like most Americans she went to the movies from childhood. What she has learned about the industry came after the assignment as critic fell to her in 1953; some of her knowledge of critical principles was acquired in the

early 1950's, when she audited a course in journalistic critical
writing at her alma mater.

She does some of the boring and exciting chores that fall to
the full-time critic. She must sift through heaps of publicity copy
and photographs from producers and distributors, and spend time
seeing motion pictures in which she has no real interest and
from which she gets little genuine enjoyment. She has to keep
an eye on the industry, for developments such as the several
varieties of wide screens and methods of projecting upon them.
Now and then she is free to go on junkets with other journalistic
critics of the cinema, but she has no time for special articles, and
in subject matter must shift from cinema to church to cooking
in a few days' time.

Hazards of the Job

Some of the pleasant aspects have been noted in telling about
Mr. Atkinson and Miss Apikian. But in considering journalistic
criticism as an occupation, even as a part-time staffer or an outside free lancer, we must look more intimately at some of the
hazards and problems. It may be, however, that certain critics
would consider these part of the fun of the critical life.

Journalistic critics are subject to assaults from outside of
journalism itself as well as from within their own occupation.
They also occasionally are dogged by bad luck. Diversity, as we
have seen, is forced upon them. Isolation is an additional psychological problem. We are not concerned here with some of
the commoner hazards, such as insufficient salary or uncomfort-
able working conditions, but this does not mean we ignore or
do not admit them as facts.

One of the more common outside hazards is described by
Milton R. Bass, who writes on music, radio-television, drama,
and books for the *Berkshire Eagle* of Pittsfield, Mass. In his
weekly column, "The Lively Arts," he has related that on one
occasion he referred facetiously to capital punishment.

"In the return mail was a letter from the Boston lady who heads
the committee to abolish capital punishment in this state," he
wrote. "She made a few pointed comments about the type of

person who would joke about a subject as serious as this one, and implied a session with a head doctor might straighten out my quirks." He mentions how necessary it is to be circumspect. It has come to the point where not only critics but all writers and all performers are fearful of offending various special pressure groups, well-meaning persons who sometimes go to extremes in defending their causes.

Attacks from outside range from prominent performers taking cracks at critics to the greater handicap of theater owners and managers excluding reviewers from the precincts. There was the remark, for instance, of Leonard Bernstein, conductor of the New York Philharmonic Orchestra, when Martin Agronsky of the National Broadcasting Company asked him his opinion of music critics. Said Bernstein, as reported by *Time:* "I have come to take them not very seriously any more. When you do get mad at a critic is when he is a self-advertised authority and at the same time proceeds to display ignorance, making mistakes, showing he doesn't have ears to hear with." And the remark of David Susskind, television producer, who said in another issue of the same magazine that television critics are "too flippant, too cursory, too gossipy, not constructive enough, and not important enough to create a body of critical judgment on one of the most important mediums ever invented."

The classic instance of interference from outsiders is the experience several drama critics have had with the Schubert theater organization, whose method of retaliation for unfavorable reviews is to take the critic off the free ticket list.[1] This befell Elliot Norton, for many years theater writer for the Boston *Post,* in 1956. He had reviewed *The Ponder Heart* unfavorably both in the daily edition and in a special Sunday article. Subsequently he had to buy a ticket in order to review the opening of *Someone Waiting* at a Schubert theater in Boston.

This incident, one of a series involving the same producers, gained national attention because a special House Judiciary

[1] Most publications and other media accept passes, review copies of books, and free discs for their critics; only a few have the policy of buying their own so as to preserve, at least theoretically, complete independence.

subcommittee was asked to investigate allegations that the Boston Schubert theaters infringed on freedom of the press, violated anti-trust laws, and put on shows "influenced by communism or containing filth." These last two charges were dropped, but the others pursued, for not only had Norton been taken off the free list but also the Schuberts had reduced their advertising in the *Post*. The paper began a front-page series giving the background of the situation. Soon Norton was restored to the list. The subcommittee criticized the Schuberts for using "economic pressures" on a critic but said there technically was no violation of guarantees of a free press.

George Jean Nathan, who had experienced such treatment years before, much earlier had shown that he was not bothered by it. A proverb in his *Testament* reads: ". . . I can't see the sense of being indignant over the exercise of any man's inalienable rights, however much of an ass I personally may consider him."

Freedom of the Critic

What freedom of expression does the American journalistic critic of any of the arts, popular or fine, possess? This question must be answered according to medium. The critic writing for newspaper, magazine, and book publication is as free as any other writers for these media. This liberty is considerable, especially by comparison with the rights of critics in many other nations, both those of the West and of Communist countries. The freest critics of all are found in most Asian lands outside China. The critic of radio or television, by reason of the fact that he has resorted to print for expression, would seem to be more restricted. This hampering is explained by the position of advertisers in relation to the various media. A newspaper or magazine editor may print what he wishes, for no self-respecting one permits an advertiser to tell him, at least directly, what he may or may not publish. But a radio or television station manager does not necessarily determine the content of his programs; offerings are decided by the sponsor. It is common for an advertiser to select the format, content, and scope of what goes into the program period he is buying. Witness the intervention, for example, of the advertiser in the content and talent of the "Hit Parade" television program or with the format offered by Gisele MacKenzie's program of 1957–58. This is taken for granted in radio and television. Such a problem does not exist for media not directly supported by advertising: motion pictures, syndicates, news services, recordings, and books.

Internal Interference

While a newspaper or magazine publisher resists direct interference from his advertisers and even sometimes his angels, many a publisher is not innocent of hamstringing his own critics.

The most direct manner, one entirely within a proprietor's rights but speaking badly for his ethics, is simply to refuse to print material adversely critical of an advertiser, of a friend, or even certain local people he wishes to protect. Related to this is the policy of treating reviews of the arts as unimportant and slashing copy according to convenience, of censoring by deletion, of suggesting that certain events need not be reviewed when the reason is obvious favoritism.

Typical of the place that critical writing has in too many ordinary newspapers is its treatment on a certain Midwestern daily of about 130,000 circulation. Book reviews are carried irregularly, only one or two in an occasional issue, dressed up more or less like news stories with no special typographical display. If a musical event occurs in the city, it is reviewed, but the review must be innocuous. Both these types of critical writing for some years were produced by the same person, a reporter who specialized in an entirely different and unrelated subject.

Recordings were reviewed for a time, but this criticism "was discontinued largely because [the reporter, another person] can't find time to do it in view of additional work recently heaped upon him through local reporting jobs," a staffer explained to the author.

Said the reporter: "However, you couldn't call anything I do 'critical writing.' Any criticism I'd make would be halted at the city desk. As, for example, in the enclosed review had I men-

tioned that Flarpa has a good voice, but the way he releases his
words gives me the jitters, it would have been cut to exactly what
it says, that Arthur Flarpa was soloist. If you can't like 'em, just
glide past 'em is our way."

Pressures from Groups

Nor do attempts at interference come only from publishers or
owners with understandable desires to present a monolithic front
to their public. They come as well from various pressure groups,
journalistic and otherwise, of which critics are obliged to take
cognizance.

Fred J. Cook, reviewing J. Edgar Hoover's book, *Masters of
Deceit,* for *The Nation,* devoted part of his review to treatment
of the book by other publications. He cited what happened to
John B. Oakes, the New York *Times Book Review*'s critic of Mr.
Hoover's volume. In another otherwise complimentary review,
Mr. Oakes declared that since the American Communist Party
was deteriorating "you may well wonder just how justified his
[Hoover's] alarm really is." He also said that there seemed at
times "a naive and . . . a slightly dated quality to the contents
of Mr. Hoover's book. . . ."

These ideas, Mr. Cook reported, "provoked an outburst."
George Sokolsky, Hearst political columnist, was so outraged by
Mr. Oakes' *lèse-majesté* that he trained a full barrage upon the
unfortunate critic. William F. Buckley, Jr., in the *National Review,* began with the theme that anyone who attacks Mr. Hoover
winds up looking terribly silly. Mr. Buckley added that "Alan
Barth of the Washington *Post* had a go at it, and the effect was
that of a teen-ager trying to impress his elders with a dirty joke."

Experienced critics often are not fazed by such reactions. Some
even relish a fight, for at least it indicates they are being read,
and the opposition may stimulate added reading. But neophytes
and thin-skinned critics suffer from them, and sometimes become
queasy and cautious about saying what they believe.

The records show that critics have been fired for their social
views, as was Ewing Poteet, drama and music reviewer of the

New Orleans *Item,* who signed a petition opposing racial segregation on the city's trolleys and buses.

Critics and Their Organizations

The feeling of isolation, a more subtle element in a critic's life, has been given little remedy. Like all journalists, critical writers for the press are likely to be individualistic. Journalists were slow to organize themselves into societies, clubs, and unions; the union movement among them was puny in the United States until 1933, when the American Newspaper Guild was formed. Critical writers on newspapers often are members of this group, but those employed by magazines are not, since this union, the only substantial one in the journalistic world, has few contracts with periodicals. Some unanimity is provided also through such groups for writers as the Society of Magazine Writers and the Authors League of America and its subsidiaries. Writers of critical articles for national magazines and books of criticism are eligible for the league.

Drama, music, and art critics have their own organizations. One which united many critics and the most exclusive, no doubt, is the New York Drama Critics Circle; Gotham is the only city sufficiently populated by critics to support such an organization. Its members include that feared group of drama critics—names like John Chapman, Walter Kerr, and Otis Guernsey are common on the roster—who are thought powerful enough to commit play murder with typewriters.

With the support and encouragement for several years of the American Symphony Orchestra League, a group was formed for music critics in 1957. Nearly fifty of them formed the Music Critics Association, taking in writers for both large and small publications. This association was an outgrowth of a series of five Music Critics Workshops sponsored by the league; a summary of the first four workshops has been published. A few small regional groups have been functioning, also.

The International Association of Art Critics has American members. Formed in 1948, its headquarters are in Paris, but generally it meets in different European cities. Like music critics, art critics have been holding workshop sessions, panel discussions, lectures, and other gatherings to discuss their functions and problems. They attend important artistic events which they later analyze in their workshops.

Editor or Critic?

Occupationally it should be clear there is a functional difference between an editor of a subject and a critic of it, even though these two positions usually are held by one person. The critic evaluates; the editor is responsible for coverage of news of the particular art, plans and makes up special or regular pages, edits copy, handles pictures, and performs other characteristic staff duties.

The differences between editors and critics are seen in the description earlier in this chapter of the duties of the critics working for the New York *Times.* Few publications can so sharply separate the editorial and critical duties. Thus anyone anticipating a career as a critic should realize that in all probability he will have to be a working journalist as well as a writer commenting on the arts. This explains why so many journalistic critics, past and present, have shared their time between the art they specialize in and general journalism. It also explains why sound preparation in a school of journalism is helpful.

Rewards of the Job

However one gets into it, journalistic criticism has its rewards as well as its headaches. The more important of the latter already have been described. The rewards, it was said, are not much in dollars. But, thanks to the general improvement in salaries in the journalistic world, neither are they niggardly.

Full-time critics for large newspapers usually work under union contracts. Since only the largest publications can afford full-timers, the salaries of these men and women are near the top of the scale for nonexecutives. Even if there is no contract, the salary still can be high, for union scale has increased the earnings on the large nonunion papers, such as the Chicago

Tribune. Writers who are part-time and on unionized papers receive salaries determined by their general classification and length of experience. A clue to these figures is the fact that the American Newspaper Guild has achieved $150 minimum weekly on many large dailies. Since part-time critics on nonunion small publications are primarily reporters or serve in some other such capacity, their earnings are less than those on the big papers with union contracts. The figures here range between $75 and $100 weekly, and differ for men and women, the latter earning less.

Generalizations cannot be made about salaries on magazines, since periodicals are almost untouched by editorial department unionism. Only about twenty magazines, most of them large, have contracts. Because even the largest are weeklies or monthlies, few of their critics are full time. They are paid widely varying salaries, and often by the article or review. Here, if they are staffers, too, their duties are diverse, and the critic may be expected to do layout, make-up, and other editorial office work.

Part-time free lancers, that is, teachers, librarians, and others whose main occupation is not writing, if they are critics for moderate-size or small dailies or weeklies or most magazines (i.e., the bulk of American publications), are paid by the word, page, or column, in passes to plays and concerts, in review copies of books or records, and in subscriptions to the paper. Word rates range from one cent in a small daily to ten cents in a small magazine; column rates vary from $1 on a small paper to $25 on a metropolitan daily. Some magazines pay by the page rather than the column, averaging from $5 to $10.

The Other Rewards

Described so far have been the main tangible rewards, but for the widely known critic they are not the only source of income from his effort. As a side line, some have gone into radio and television (Deems Taylor and Clifton Fadiman, for example); published their criticisms in book form (Edwin F. Edgett, Olin Downes, Llewellyn Jones, Deems Taylor, Harold Clurman,

Wolcott Gibbs, George Bernard Shaw, to mention only a very few); written books on criticism itself (Oscar Thompson, Francis Hackett, John Macy, George Jean Nathan, Llewellyn Jones); become lecturers (John Mason Brown); and won appointments to university faculties (Granville Hicks, Oscar Thompson).

One of the intangible or psychic rewards of the life of the journalistic critic already has been mentioned in another connection: its prestige. The height probably has been achieved by Atkinson. *Variety* once told this story: When curtain time came one night a little theater group in San Francisco did not go on with the play. After twenty minutes the director came out onto the stage and told the audience that he was sorry for the delay "but we're waiting for Brooks Atkinson . . . who promised to be here tonight." Quietly a voice from the rear of the room said: "I've been here all the time," and at once the curtain went up on the play.

Another is association with the noted and the notorious. Robert Sylvester, of the New York *Daily News* drama department, reported a few years ago that "Part of my duties, while working my head to the bone for the *News,* is to meet famous actors, famous press agents, and famous bop musicians in famous saloons. It is a hard life but I love it. The most famous saloon is the one called '21' and I don't make this one more than twice a year. Last week I made it twice, once right after the other, and the delirium is still upon me. How much gracious living can a country boy want?"

Most writers are more at home writing about the subjects on which they are specialists, for they have confidence in what they produce. This satisfaction is granted the critic, whereas the general reporter, administrative editor, copy editor of a newspaper, or associate or assistant editor, or some other general functionary of a magazine shifts from subject to subject and finally becomes master of none. The achievement of a measure of expertness is another reward for critics.

The Influence of the Critic

Another important reward is that of being an influence. This is more than gratification of a critic's ego or of his sincere desire munity orchestras in the United States and the annual classical music receipts which now exceed those of baseball; [the] swiftly paced popularity of ballet, due in large extent to dance on television." To these he could have added the huge public interest in photography.

to be of use. It is vital in deciding the place, importance, and validity of critical writing in general. Even if such writing had no other effect than to provide an outlet for the impressions and expressions of writers, it would be justified. Since it also has an obvious effect upon the arts themselves, upon spectators of the arts, and upon journalism as well, it must be accepted as more than a passing reward for the critic.

Our knowledge of the impact of critical writing is spotty; it would be difficult to measure in any systematic way. Also, the effect has been undependable. Take, for example, the influence of drama critics. In New York City, if the writers for the big dailies and a few influential weeklies (*Variety*, in particular) condemn a play, it is likely to fail, but not always. *Abie's Irish Rose* is the stock example of critical misfire. In many a smaller city the local drama critics' views are ignored. Similarly with books. But it is easy to quote exceptions and safer to go on the policy that since the definition of success for a book, play, movie, or television show has not been agreed upon (it may be commercial or artistic or both), criticism should be considered an art and not a science. Results, therefore, cannot be accurately measured.

Critics can help mold the careers of artists. Kirsten Flagstad, the Norwegian opera star, was unknown in the United States, but New York's music critics immediately spotted her magnificent voice when she made her first American appearance at a matinee on February 2, 1935, with the Metropolitan. She sang the part of "Sieglinde" in *Die Walküre*. The next day she was hailed by both Lawrence Gilman of the *Tribune* and Olin Downes of the *Times*. Later in the week she appeared as "Isolde" and those two leading music critics were joined by Samuel Chotzinoff (*Post*), W. J. Henderson (*Sun*), A. J. Liebling (*Journal-American*), Francis Perkins (also *Herald Tribune*), Winthrop Sargeant (*Journal-American* also), and others. As a result, Miss Flagstad became recognized as one of the world's leading sopranos.

Lack of critical appreciation, on the other hand, has discouraged permanently some creative artists who could not afford to go on writing or painting without critical acclaim and the financial success that sometimes accompanies it. The author knows of a number of talented young people, some his own former students, who in their college days or soon thereafter were capable poets and novelists. But most of them ceased writing because they were neglected or misjudged by the critics. A leading book publisher, for instance, issued a collection of poems. He advertised it more widely than is usual with such a book. It received only moderate, although approving, critical attention, but scarcely the space and position allotted to a new volume by a popular mystery story writer. For this the public is in part to blame, but the critics sometimes cater too much to the public. Later the poet became one of the most highly paid male clothing advertisement models and no longer writes. Others turned to nursing, radio and television announcing, teaching, public relations work, and straight editorial labor for newspapers and magazines, and ceased to be fully creative as writers.

The type of influence to which many critics aspire but few achieve is that wielded by prominent newspaper and magazine writers, such as Jack Gould and John Crosby. They are more influential than almost any critic who occasionally succeeds in directing attention to some book, play, movie, or art show which he esteems or condemns. So influential have Gould and Crosby become that *Newsweek* once dubbed them, along with a few others, as the "new elite" of the newsrooms. This distinction, if so it is, was restricted to television critics, but there are dozens more from the other arts who could join them. The magazine added Terrence O'Flaherty of the San Francisco *Chronicle*, Ben Gross, New York *Daily News;* Janet Kern, Chicago *American;* Jack O'Brian, Hearst Syndicate; and Harriet Van Horne, Scripps-Howard Newspapers. These and others, the newsmagazine reported, were in 1957 receiving 600 letters a week. The influence of Gould and Crosby was reported to be especially heavy upon the "upper echelons of the networks" because the main offices of the chains are in New York, where their papers are published. Briefly, in fact, Gould was hired by the Columbia Broadcasting System because of his judgment, but the critic was not happy as a network executive and returned to his daily stint in journalism.

An example of Gould's direct influence on television occurred

in the fall of 1956 when he complained because only one United States television station carried the United Nations debate on the crisis when Britain, France, and Israel invaded Egypt. He called the networks "stupid, selfish, and irresponsible." By the end of the week all three had increased their coverage substantially. *Newsweek* quoted one producer as saying that "For 48 hours Gould was running CBS and NBC."

For a Better Occupation

What critical writing needs in order to become a still more attractive occupation depends largely upon the conduct and taste of the American reading and listening public. Publishers would allot more space, hire more full-time critics, and pay better salaries and rates to their present ones, if they thought the public culturally mature enough to demand more and better critical writing and speaking, or if more advertising came from the world of the arts.

But even if the publishers and station managers are right in their appraisal of public taste, journalism cannot wait for the public to catch up with it. It also must act as an educator and seek to arouse greater interest in literature, music, and the other arts. It has done this to a degree with sports, science, and home-making. Such altruism, unfortunately, under a system of publishing for profit in order to assure existence, can go only so far. Owners and publishers of newspapers and magazines and operators of radio and television stations possibly are not aware of the great increase in the practice of and interest in the arts among the American people. A little study of museum attendance figures, establishment and patronage of symphony orchestra concerts and other musical events, number and sales of books of all types might indicate that the public is ready for more criticism of the arts than it was a half century ago.

Donald D. Key, music and art critic for the Cedar Rapids (Iowa) *Gazette,* writing in *The Quill* in 1958, cited in support of this point the "Thousands of week-end painters whose works may not be great but whose interest grows . . . and whose enthusiasm is contagious to associates; [the] more than 1,000 com-

Background for Criticism

Should a critic have special training and experience in the subject he criticizes? Before setting down his judgment of the work of others, should he also study critical writing?

It may seem nonsense even to raise these questions, for what sort of critic is he who lacks background? Unfortunately, critics devoid of adequate preparation are not rare in journalistic circles.

Stanley Meisler, in surveying the careers and activities of entertainment editors of moderate-size dailies, observed that "The most obvious fact gleaned from results of the questionnaire is that editors, with rare exceptions, do not expect entertainment writers to have special training." Since "entertainment editors" includes critics of drama, movies, books, and other arts, this statement brings out why it is not so unreasonable to raise the questions at the opening of this chapter. Editors and publishers for years have been tolerating ignorance in their critics and tacitly encouraging it by their tolerance.

Mr. Meisler found that of twenty-one writers on music, two had had musical training, one had operated a dance hall, another had managed a record store, and one had been a symphony orchestra official. No other field of the arts was so well represented, he pointed out. "This suggests," he went on to say, that "editors sometimes feel anyone can cover theater, movies, radio, television, and nightclubs but somebody musical is needed for music." He wrote this in spite of the fact that only two had knowledge of music and only three others some connection with the world of music.

Henri Temianka, writing in *Esquire* about music critics from an unusual viewpoint, since he was a concert violinist, related

that a music critic of what he called "one of the leading newspapers in the Northwest" once asked to interview him. Instead
he interviewed the critic. This was the result:

"How long have you been a music critic?" he asked.

"Three months," was the answer.

"What did you do before that?"

"Sports reporter."

"What training have you had in music?"

"None."

"Why did you get the job?"

"Because they needed a music critic right away."

Mr. Temianka did not present this as typical, but the situation
described is evidently not unusual and has been so for many
years, as any teacher of journalism can affirm because of the
letters he receives from former students suddenly pressed into
critical duty.

A color-blind art critic can do nothing about his affliction,
although he can do something about his conscience. But the
ignorant critic or the one unaware that there are standards and
principles of criticism can remedy his shortcoming. And, as an
examination of their careers shows, the outstanding critics,
through observation and study, if not formal schooling, equip
themselves properly. It is one thing to be thrown into a new
job and assume one can handle it adequately, and it is another
to be tossed into it, become aware of one's deficiencies, and set
about overcoming them.

The Paths to Criticism

An examination of the biographies of several critics, largely
serving American newspapers and magazines, shows that they
found their way into their work with various degrees of background knowledge and training. It would be pleasant, but impossible, to record that no eminent critic has written until he
was fully prepared. Some started from a purely journalistic background; others knew no journalism but were well informed on,
even practitioners of, their art.

John Rosenfield, movie-music-theater critic for the Dallas

(Tex.) *News,* a leading daily of the Southwest, described his path to his present post in the summer, 1953, issue of the *Southwest Review* in an article, "Learning to Be a Critic." He was covering city hall for the paper in 1925 when the sports editor decided to quit. Rosenfield and Chauncey Brown, who had been handling stage, screen, and music, both applied for the sports job, for it paid $5 a week more.

Brown got the sports job and, as Rosenfield put it, "We got Chauncey's job 'handling' stage, screen, and music whenever the city desk did not have anything more pressing. The city desk seldom did."

By the late 1950's Rosenfield had reached the point where he was known nationally as the leading critic in the Southwest. Mrs. Aline Jean Treanor, art critic of the *Daily Oklahoman* and Oklahoma *City Times,* summarized a common view when she wrote to the author:

"You should know, and must do so, that John Rosenfield is the critic without peer in this part of the country. That is, he is the critic of most power and influence, and he writes well, too . . . has a good mind, and a smattering of all the arts, and he has built his power well. Pretty much of what Dallas is, it owes to Rosenfield, artistically speaking."

From another source comes the substantiating account of the time one of the big symphony orchestras of the nation was contracted to go to another Texas city than Dallas. Rosenfield, always eager for Dallas to have the best, created such a local stir about this neglect that the orchestra changed its itinerary to take in that center of Southwestern culture.

The late Burton Rascoe was one of the most versatile of critics and proved in his own career that critical principles can be applied across the board to the various arts, for he was a capable reviewer of books, a drama critic, and radio-television critical columnist (much like Gilbert Seldes, now known for his television criticism but earlier identified with the arts in general). Rascoe came into the critical world via straight journalism, as he relates in his autobiographical book, *Before I Forget.*

Originally a Kansan, as a boy he lived in Oklahoma. While

in high school he worked as a reporter, editorial writer, and columnist for the Shawnee (Okla.) *Herald*. He enrolled at the University of Chicago and paid part of his way by working as campus correspondent for newspapers. He left school before graduation to work full time on the Chicago *Tribune*, which by 1919 had him serving, simultaneously, as drama critic, assistant Sunday editor, rotogravure editor, opposite-editorial page editor, and chief critic for the Saturday book-review page.

Rascoe then went into magazine work at *McCall's*; after a few years as an associate editor, he reverted to newspaper work by becoming for seven years literary editor of the New York *Tribune*. But he also served during this period as editor of *The Bookman* magazine, one of the few periodicals then largely devoted to critical writing. His criticism jobs from that time are too many to record here. As a columnist he appeared in four hundred newspapers. He wrote criticism for the Literary Guild, *Arts and Decoration, Vanity Fair,* New York *Sun, Esquire, Newsweek, American Mercury,* and the New York *World-Telegram*. At his death he was conducting a syndicated radio-television column for newspapers. He also taught playwrighting and was the author of eight books, several dealing with literary criticism.

A critic whose career long antedated Rascoe's was Edwin F. Edgett. During forty-four years on the now extant famous Boston daily, the *Evening Transcript*, he was drama and then literary critic. After Edgett left Harvard he took a $5-a-week job writing about the theater for the weekly *Beacon* in Boston. Earlier he had published free-lance pieces in small Boston papers as well as the *Journal* and the *Transcript*. Edgett, he explains in his autobiography, found that, while moneywise this was of no importance, it gave him free admission to theaters, an outlet for his views, and finally, in 1894, at the age of 27, the job he really wanted. Francis H. Jenks, drama editor of the *Transcript*, died suddenly. Edgett had written little for him. The day after Jenks' death William E. Bryant, drama editor of the Boston *Journal*, asked Edgett why he did not apply for Jenks' place. This encouraged him; he applied and soon got the position. Presumably Edgett's Harvard undergraduate studies were helpful by way of preparation, but they cannot account for the position of eminence he later attained as a critic.

From even less auspicious beginnings came C. J. Bulliet, who was art critic of the Chicago *Daily News* and later for the Chicago *Evening Post*. He began as a police reporter in Louisville, Ky., did the same job on the Indianapolis *Star,* became a theater press agent for nine years, switched to art, and spent most of his journalistic career as art critic until his death. His only claim to knowing anything about his subject, he said, was that he was of a French family. He was author of several books on painting, one of which, *Apples and Madonnas,* was widely noted and one of the first, by an American art critic, to be hospitable to the impressionists.

Although the late Wolcott Gibbs also came out of a newsman's background, he shook off the deleterious effects of newspaper work (hasty writing, lack of time for careful investigation in producing routine news accounts, and too-easy publication) sufficiently to become not only one of the country's most penetrating drama critics but also an essayist and dramatist, a precise and original craftsman with words, and an effective satirist. After three years of railroad work he went into newspaperdom on a small Long Island daily, shifting to *The New Yorker* in the mid-1920's as a deskman, when he was 25 and the magazine only two years old. He became a writer of virtually all the many types of material that sophisticated weekly publishes. Gibbs succeeded Robert Benchley as drama critic in 1940, producing in his 18 years at the post honest and often biting criticism. As modest as one of his predecessors at *The New Yorker,* Alexander Woollcott, was not, he is quoted as once having said: "I've always felt that play criticism was a silly occupation for a grown man."

Not unlike these backgrounds were or are those of Claudia Cassidy, the bristling music critic of the Chicago *Tribune* (one magazine article called her "The Queen of Culture" and discussed her "reign of terror"); the late Richard L. Stokes, who was drama and music critic for the St. Louis *Post-Dispatch,* music critic for the New York *Evening World,* playwright, librettist, lecturer, and Washington correspondent; Robert Sensenderfer, who died in

the mid-1950's and who became known as the dean of Philadelphia drama critics. Of Sensenderfer it may be noted that he
reversed the usual trend by going from a long career as play
reviewer to sports editor (Philadelphia *Bulletin*).

Also coming through the newspaper channel was another drama
critic and playwright who died in the mid-1950's at about the
same time as Stokes and Sensenderfer. This was Robert Garland,
who started as a Baltimore *News* feature writer and within two
years became drama editor and critic for the *American* of the
same city, and later served similarly on other Baltimore and on
New York papers, and wrote criticism for the *Music Record*.

Other Careers

From the realm of movie reviewers comes the story of Brad
Darrach, Jr., principal critic of that art for *Time* magazine. When
he began his work with the newsmagazine, he had been an
insurance investigator and a newspaperman. In general this is
the pattern for many more. Harriet Van Horne, television critic
for the Scripps-Howard Newspapers, was first a newspaper reporter; Bob Sublette began by writing about football and was a
newspaper librarian, church editor, sports writer, police reporter,
and book reviewer for seven years before he began radio-television writing for the New Orleans *States*. The late Joseph Henry
Jackson, who became a leading critical writer on the Pacific
Coast, was first an advertising man and then editor of *Sunset*
magazine, before he began his long career as a journalistic critic
of books. Clara Hieronymous, art and drama critic for the Nashville *Tennessean*, has an extraordinary background. She taught
social problems and sociology at the University of Tulsa, was at
the same time a labor market analyst and earned master's degrees
in both business administration and social work.

And so it goes. Fanny Butcher, literary editor of the Chicago
Tribune, began book reviewing from her college classes. The
only background George Jean Nathan had for the lifetime career
he made of drama criticism was his activity in dramatics at
Cornell. William Hogan, Joseph Henry Jackson's replacement on
the San Francisco *Chronicle*, worked on the paper's copydesk
and had done military journalism before he became drama and

film editor. Roy H. Copperud, who writes music criticism as part of his work for the Stockton (Calif.) *Record,* has a varied background, but none of it musical. Once, according to *Editor & Publisher,* for which he writes regularly on lexicography, he was asked what his qualifications were for his criticism. He answered: "If you read my reviews you would know that I have no qualifications."

The neophyte who is encouraged by knowing that one can achieve critical distinction, locally if not nationally and often nationally as well, without necessarily having elaborate training will be pleased to know more about the careers of Jack Gould, chief radio-television critic of the New York *Times,* and John Crosby, his counterpart on the New York *Herald Tribune.* Generally they are thought to be among the most skillful critics of these media in the country; critics elsewhere read them as models.

Neither is a college graduate. Both got their first journalistic experience writing about Broadway for the *Herald Tribune.* Gould did his first critical writing after serving as second-string dramatic critic for the *Times;* Crosby went into the business of writing about radio after a five-year interval in military service. As *Newsweek* has reported it: "The editors had no room for him in his old craft [covering the Broadway beat]. They shunted him off 'behind the classified ads' with the suggestion that he try writing a radio column. Grudgingly he did, though he knew nothing about radio, did not even own a set." As this book is being written his column appears in 103 newspapers with an estimated readership of 15 million, he writes for national magazines, has turned out books, ventured into television, and draws a salary of $40,000.

With all of these critics and many others like them, it was the art form they dealt with that suffered during their apprenticeship. But they all were obliged to teach themselves while on the job.

Knowing the Art First

Another group chose not to do it the hard way but to obtain background—through experience, study, or both—before going on the critical journalism job. And this group not surprisingly also includes many widely known and distinguished names. Typical is the career of Ward Morehouse, drama critic and playwright. As a boy in Savannah, Ga., where he was born early in this century, Morehouse demonstrated his devotion to the theater by writing plays and setting up an amateur theater group in which he also acted. By his sixteenth year he had written twenty dramas. When his father offered him a place in his manufacturing business, Ward said no, that he wanted to be a playwright and to travel.

He became a tragedian's assistant, roaming through the South with this old-fashioned Shakespearean actor, who gave readings wherever they could wangle him an engagement. Financially this was a failure; Morehouse relates in one of his autobiographical books that one day he was left stranded with $1.65 and too much pride to ask for money from his parents. He took a railroad job until he earned enough cash to go home. There he declared: "I've decided I'm going to be a newspaperman. I might even become a dramatic critic." As it turned out, he became both.

He went to work in 1915 for the Savannah *Press*, as reporter, asking for the chance and saying that he would work for nothing for six months. In three he was on the payroll, at $9 a week. He ushered in theaters so he could see the plays that came from the North. In seven months he was taken on by the Atlanta *Journal* at $17.50. He covered police news first, but soon became play reporter and then put out the Sunday magazine section. He was 19. He covered movies as well as plays. Then he decided to go to New York for a newspaper job. Why?

"The truth is," he told another *Journal* man, "I just want to go to New York, to be in New York, to live in New York, to work in New York."

"What the hell has New York got that we haven't got right here?"

"I'll tell you," he said. "It has the theater. It has theaters. It has plays running all the time, dozens of plays. Thousands of actors. I'll be within a subway ride of thirty, forty, fifty theaters. I'll be on Broadway."

Off North he went, got a job as a reporter on the New York

Tribune, and soon had a theater column to write. He saw six or seven plays a week, sometimes four on a weekend. He came to know the famous people of the theater, was both insulted and helped by Alexander Woollcott, and also had some success selling short stories and writing plays. Three were produced: *Gentlemen of the Press, Miss Quix,* and *New York Town.* In 1926 he transferred to the drama department of the New York *Sun.* For 24 years he wrote a daily theater column; during the final eight he also wrote criticisms. When the *Sun* was sold in 1950, Morehouse immediately was taken on by the paper with which it was merged: the New York *World-Telegram.* There he continued his reviewing until 1954. That year he began a theater column for the North American Newspaper Alliance, where he is at this writing. Sometime in the early 1950's he took a year out to move to Colorado Springs to run a small paper, but he became too lonely for New York's theater life and the opportunity to express his views on the new plays.

Morehouse brought firsthand experience gained in boyhood to his early critical writing. Another writer, among the most widely respected critics, also laid the background for this work as a child. This is Winthrop Sargeant, music critic for *The New Yorker* and a *Life* magazine staff member (where his writing does not deal with music). Sargeant was a musical prodigy. At ten he conducted the San Francisco People's Symphony Orchestra in his own composition, then was violinist in orchestras conducted by Toscanini, Rodzinski, Walter, and Damrosch, studied music in three countries, and also played in dance bands and worked on Broadway show scores. He has been music editor for United Press International news service and has written on music for many magazines.

Another Time, Inc. staffer, Wilder Hobson, who headed *Time* magazine's music department for some years, was a trombonist and became a music historian, writing a book on American jazz. A later music critic for the same newsmagazine, Carter Harman, was a clarinetist at nine, a major in music at Princeton, and winner of a music fellowship that kept him at the university after graduation. After a dramatic military career in World War II, he wrote on music for the New York *Times,* and then became a *Time* critic. A look at the biographies of Walter Kerr, New York *Herald Tribune* drama critic, and of Maurice Dolbier, book critic for the same paper, shows similar sound backgrounding in their respective arts.

There are critics on papers outside New York and other big cities who similarly have solid backgrounds in their respective arts. Donald D. Key, fine-arts editor of the Cedar Rapids *Gazette,* a small Iowa daily noted for the high-quality journalists it has produced, was a major in music at the State University of Iowa. During his military service in World War II, he was a member of the GI Symphony Orchestra in Europe. After discharge he played the first French horn with the Houston Symphony Orchestra. He returned to the university to complete his degree and there did news work and music criticism for the *Daily Iowan.* He moved from it to the *Gazette,* where he shares his time between critical writing, editorial writing, and being assistant to the editor. His story is similar to that of critics on other small dailies—for example, Milton R. Bass, entertainment editor of the *Berkshire Eagle* of Pittsfield, Mass.

Bass came originally from the city where he now is. His college work was premedical and literary; he still is working on his dissertation. He studied piano as a child and, having become accustomed to the research approach, has learned much about music in that way, especially jazz. He writes radio-television, music, book, and art criticism for his paper, one noted for its generous space allotted to the arts, and contributes to *High Fidelity* magazine.

To such careers can be added the stories of other well-prepared critics of the present or past: the late Felix Borowski, music critic for several Chicago dailies; the late Arthur Abell, a contemporary of his, who wrote music criticism for such newspapers and magazines as *Musical Courier, Etude,* and the New York *Times;* T. H. Wenning, drama reviewer for *Newsweek,* who earlier was an actor in New York and a script writer in Hollywood; Richard C. Beatty, full-time literary editor of the Nashville *Tennessean,* who was professor of English at Vanderbilt University, a Guggenheim Foundation fellowship winner, and is author of various books in his field; Isaac Rosenfeld, who died at only 38 in 1956 after a short career as novelist, critic, and university teacher, during which he had been a reviewer for *The New Republic, The New Leader,* and the New York *Times Book Review.*

One of the great art critics of our time has written so little that has appeared in journalism that he is scarcely known to the general public: Bernard Berenson. Most of his work has appeared in his thirty books on art. He is a master of art analysis and has devoted his lifetime (at this writing he is 93) to the study of painting.

What Background Is Needed?

To debate the proposition that background is essential would appear unnecessary. All the capable critics acquire it in some way by the time they become influential. To function without it is to be a fraud; no perceptive reader is long fooled. The more important question, then, is: what background shall be obtained and how? This must be answered differently for the young person with aspirations and the shaping of his career before him and for the mature man or woman who must get the grounding while doing work related to critical writing, such as another sort of journalism.

What background either the beginner or the person with a start must obtain has been suggested by numerous critics and artists. Sometimes their observations deal only with one of the arts, but what they say frequently is true for all of them.

Christopher Fry, writing as a dramatist who has had an "experience of critics" (the title of the book in which the quotation to follow appears), says that the critic must have "a subtle understanding of playwriting, acting and production, so that a fault shall not be laid at the wrong door . . . He must have the patience and concentration of a bird-watcher, the eye of a sleuth, the capacity for experience of an explorer. . . ."

The critic, as well, should have an analytical mind. When reviewing a book, for instance, he should ask, as S. Stevenson Smith recommends in his *The Craft of the Critic,* such questions as: "How were these effects achieved? How was the work put together? What technical devices did the author use? How did his imagination function to produce effects so remarkable? What idea lies behind his work?"

One of England's most noted writers, who was novelist, political theorist, and author of five books on the theater, as well as the drama critic of the distinguished London *Observer,* gave his definition of the ideal critic which reveals some of the background he must possess. Ivor Brown wrote: "I believe that the ideal critic is an enthusiastic introducer. True, he must dismiss the shoddy as such. But his primary function is not to go slamming about the place and showing what a bright boy he is, but to act as a persuasive, not a dictatorial, guide. He can dismiss his dislikes briefly; his admirations he should communicate as fully as possible in these days of scanty space."

Martin Mayer, American free-lance article writer and book author, has said that the "ideal critic is a self-centered, vain, arrogant nuisance who finds 'what is put before him,' as Mencken put it 'infinitely less interesting than what is within him.' "

Philip Hope-Wallace, another noted English critic, who wrote for the Manchester *Guardian* and several magazines, believed that a drama critic ought to have an eye for detail. Coming down to specifics, he said that the critic should be capable of re-creating on the page what he has seen and heard on the stage, "and at the same time convey the emotional impression it has made on him. . . ." Eric Keown, for many years drama critic for *Punch,* differed from some of his colleagues about the amount of knowledge a critic should possess. He believed that the writer cannot be expected to know all about the theater and saw no reason why he should, "for he is not concerned with how things are done but only with their effect on his senses." The qualifications he listed in *An Experience of Critics* are succinct: the critic should be "an intelligent playgoer who has trained himself to absorb impressions as accurately as possible; who, by reading and experience, has acquired certain ideals of taste and developed a background against which he can sort out these impressions and put them into perspective; and can pass them on coherently."

An American music critic, Robert C. Marsh of the Chicago *Sun-Times,* believes that the sort of knowledge a critic needs "is almost certain to be found only in persons of diversified interests who have worked in the area in which they are to function critically long before they ever had a thought of doing so professionally," he wrote the author.

Mr. Marsh cited as an example his criticisms of the performances at the Ravinia Festival, the music center on Chicago's North Shore. "I shall be writing about a summer music center I have attended regularly for twenty years, without any idea—even through the final season before my appointment to the *Sun-Times* —that it would become a professional concern."

He then sets a requirement that may seem stern to beginners: "In other words, no one who is unwilling to invest ten years of his life into an area without any guarantee of getting anything back except personal satisfaction is likely to secure the background a critic must have. For criticism, more than most types of writing, is based on love of one's subject. Unless one can keep the freshness and interest that people only have—in most cases—when they're doing things for fun, criticism can be as deadly and unrewarding an area as any in which a writer must function."

Martin Mayer also said, in the section on criticism in *The Writer's Craft,* a book by Frederic A. Birmingham, that the first requirement for an aspiring critic is, of course, "the critical instinct, which usually develops young . . . Second . . . is a feeling for words and their precise use . . . Knowledge of the subject is necessary, too . . . To escape dryness, a critic also should know as much as he can absorb about the general intellectual climate of the time." To these he added the willingness to make judgments that "history may prove false."

The critic's qualifications, then, come down to this: he must like what he does, have an absorbing interest in the art form itself, possess an understanding (although not necessarily great competence as a performer) of the art form, have the ability to transmit in words his reactions and judgments, and, as W. C. Brownell put it, know more than his subject, "for no one knows his subject who knows his subject alone."

Obtaining the Background

A book five times the size of this could not provide the background of historical facts on even one of the fine or popular arts, much less all of them. The student critic or the working one seeking to build a body of knowledge cannot expect to find it compressed into a dozen easy lessons. The beginner can major in the arts in his college work. As an undergraduate he can couple such study with liberal arts and journalism training. As a postgraduate he can do advanced work, through the doctorate if he wishes, or enroll in an art school. The practicing critic who senses a gap in his education but finds even evening school classes more than his schedule will accommodate can give himself a course of reading, beginning perhaps with some of the basic volumes on the arts. What he teaches himself about music or painting cannot, of course, come solely from books. Reading must be accompanied by observation and listening; that is, by listening to records and tapes, visiting museums, reading catalogues and guides, attending recitals and concerts of music and the dance, going to movies, and watching television.

Even the background of criticism is elaborate, for as a profession it is an activity at least two centuries old. As the bibliography of this book shows, there is study of criticism itself that can be done without too much searching, but it should cover not only the books on it but also the living examples from the best publications of the time.

The amount of work in such seeking after background is great. Jacques Barzun, in his introduction to *The Later Ego* by the late James Agate, the English drama critic, points out that "By dint of hard work after business hours he forged a technique and style that he could rely on, besides learning the history of the theatre, of actors and acting, and of British and French dramatic criticism."

It should be noted that Agate "forged a technique and

style. . . ." Such forging can be expedited by study of writing, a function which capably taught journalism and writing courses constantly perform.

To obtain elementary journalistic skills is not difficult in the United States, most of whose universities and colleges offer courses in journalistic or other writing. To receive training in critical writing *per se* is more difficult: this fact is a major justification for the present book and the chapters devoted to the writing of various types of critical copy. Courses in critical writing are relatively few in comparison to those given over to straight news reporting, magazine or feature article writing, or editorial writing. These few deal either with journalistic criticism and are available mainly in the larger schools of journalism or, more commonly, with literary criticism and are to be found in the curricula of English departments. The latter courses generally are devoted heavily to aesthetic theory, which is invaluable in giving the journalistic critic perspective and good judgment, although the journalist's readers may show little appreciation for his aesthetic sense; overindulgence in its expression may, in fact, cut the journalistic critic off from those who otherwise might read him. He should be informed about aesthetic theory but refrain from trying to take his readers too far into its abstractions.

The Philosophies of Criticism

All but the most erudite of journalistic critics can be given a severe case of mental paralysis simply by being asked a few questions:

"What are your standards of criticism?"

"What philosophy of criticism do you follow?"

"Do you consider yourself an authoritarian or an impressionistic critic?"

In corresponding with or talking to scores of critics who write for newspapers and magazines, the author of this book has rarely encountered any who are well-informed about the philosophies of criticism or have formulated standards for themselves. If they have done so, they are products of classroom or self-imposed study of philosophy, aesthetics, or criticism. But usually they have only the barest notion of these matters.

This chapter, it should be understood at once, will set up no rules nor list any collection of standards which, if met, might produce a well-grounded, full-blown critic. This is no how-to-do-it critical thinking and writing kit.

Consciously or unconsciously, each critic evolves a concept of what he thinks is a competent performance in the area he criticizes. It may be a single work from the past. It may be a changing pattern, altering as what is produced in his own time also changes. It may even be a mental concept of which he is not fully aware. A statement by Henri Peyre, the Franco-American literary scholar, applies here: "Impressionism and relativism must always play a considerable part in any critical appreciation. Taste, flair, and intention remain, after all, the least fallible asset of any appraiser of art and literature. Even more than poets, critics are born, not made."

The subject of the philosophies of criticism can no more be dealt with completely in a single chapter of a short book than the topic of theology can be treated adequately in sixteen pages of a small volume. This chapter merely attempts to describe the condition that exists in the realm of journalistic criticism and suggests what might be learned from the practices of the best journalistic critics and of those whose work was done for more permanent publications than newspapers and popular magazines.

The Uses of the Philosophies

In America, journalistic critics range from those whose only standards are their own reactions (a legitimate philosophy, although a disputed one, as we shall see) to those who judge everything in, as Norman Foerster has put it in his *Toward Standards*, "the light of the forces animating contemporary civilization. . . ."

The journalists who have studied the complexities of the philosophy of criticism and have penetrated the abstractions of aesthetic theory are engaged in doing critical writing only for that wing known as the scholarly and literary journals or other specialized periodicals. There appear to be scholars who do daily book reviewing, music criticism, or some other journalistic critical writing, but their immersion in the theories of aesthetics and the methodologies of criticism is disguised or left quietly in the background. They have come away from the intellectual adventure. Its effect upon them is below the surface of their writing, where, of course, it should be. It has made them more perceptive, conscientious, erudite, and tolerant, perhaps, but in their journalism they dare not indulge in much direct reference to it lest they lose their readers, most of whom are unaware of the critical theories and the battles that go on between exponents of various schools (although, to be sure, the really great wars were fought in the early part of the century).

This chapter at least should convince the neophyte critic that if he wants to bring the best of himself to his critical writing, whether in journalism or in longer-lasting outlets for his views, he must someday find his way intellectually through the background of criticism as well as of the particular subject matter with which he deals. There is no easy road to knowledge of the history and development of criticism as an intellectual exercise. To pretend to offer a digest thereof would invite distortion and oversimplification, although an H. G. Wells, who compressed human history into a single volume, might accomplish it.

The futility of a crash program in the study of criticism is made clear by the following considerations. Suppose a reviewer is writing about a book by one of the beat generation of writers. The critic declares it to be badly written. What does that mean? Does it mean careless grammar, unclear sentences, and misuse of words? Do such infractions make the work inferior? If so, to what? Who declares that these characteristics are necessarily bad? As soon as he makes the judgment, the critic is referring to standards set up outside himself. Another critic, however, may ignore what the first one considers faults; he may even regard them as virtues, as witness some of the reviews of books by Jack Kerouac, James Jones, and Allen Ginsburg. Must not the critic, therefore, decide at least for the time being that he considers form (let "form" cover pattern, clarity, and the like) important or unimportant? And from what within him comes the decision? From the development of a philosophy of criticism, from saying to himself, one day, "I simply cannot consider excellent a book (or play or whatever art is being criticised) that is slovenly in form; I will not give it the highest praise and it must have other qualities to overcome this limitation." Or he may decide, when reflecting casually upon his duties as critic, "I am not going to let such academic matters as sentence structure, logical plot, and accuracy make me condemn a work of art that is great in concept."

No intellectually alive critic, of course, fixes on a philosophy from which he never varies; he may in fact shift from the hard and fast attitude of authoritarianism to the freedom of impressionism and back again, or during his lifetime swing in any number of directions within these areas.

Each critic has certain standards he thinks important, barely expressed or conceived as they may be. The critic must realize that the reader (or listener or viewer) usually takes his choice among criticism and critics (often, alas, as he reads only those he agrees with, as he does in politics, instead of exposing himself to different viewpoints). Critic Jones must know he is read or heeded because he thinks verisimilitude important, for example, and that Critic Smith is read because Smith demands a spiritual quality in the arts, or Critic Brown because Brown is sure a work of art must have larger significance than mere realism, or Critic Thompson because he applies moral standards to the arts.

The critic, like the reader, does not know which is right, nor, with certainty, does anyone else. It may not be important for anyone to be right, whatever "right" means. To the reader it appears that the methods which achieve the purposes of criticism he desires are acceptable and it behooves the critic to remember that.

The Theories of Criticism

The theories of criticism are the points of view or the approach of the critic to his subject. To the police reporter of a year's journalistic experience, suddenly turned loose to criticize television or motion pictures for a small daily (no uncommon occurrence), the idea that there is a philosophy of criticism doubtless is news. He may, in time, come to agree with Stephen Pepper's insistence, in his book *The Basis of Criticism in the Arts,* that ". . . good criticism . . . is criticism based on a good philosophy . . . a good philosophy is simply the best disposition of all evidence available."

And a further point by Pepper should cause to hesitate both the police reporter turned critic and the city or managing editor who made the assignment. In the same book he writes: "A thoroughly competent critic is one who has both an intimate experience with the art he is judging and possession of reliable criteria of criticism. He may or may not be conscious of the grounds on which his criteria are supported, just as a man who uses a tool may or may not know how it is manufactured."

Assuming, then, that competent criticism begins with some theory, philosophy, approach, or point of view, we are ready to examine the better-known theories. Naturally there are no theories of reviewing, for the reviewer, in a literal sense, does his job as does any other reporter. He takes notes on firsthand events, consults biographical source books for facts about artists, familiarizes himself with the catalogues, asks the artists direct questions about their views, talks to the people scanning the exhibits, requests officials to give estimates of attendance, inquires about special events, incidents, or whatever else may make interesting copy that does not enter the arena of criticism. His philosophy of writing is that of the best journalism: objectivity, accuracy, completeness, attractiveness of presentation. He is a combination reporter and feature writer.

But the critic cannot stop there, for if he does so he avoids his main task of guiding the reader or listener and expressing himself or, as Matthew Arnold put it in his description of criticism itself: enabling himself to "know the best that is known and thought in the world and by in its turn making this known, to create a current of true and fresh ideas." In those portions of his material in which he, too, reports he must, of course, meet the standards of competent reporting. He, also, must spell the artist's name correctly, quote accurately the titles of his paintings, and not place the exhibit at Madison Square Garden if it is being held at Macy's. But what governs the content of his article is not journalism's tradition of answering the five W's and the H. It is meeting the obligation put upon him by a public that turns to him for more than objective facts.

The critical theories of the day are many and sometimes complex. They are interwoven with philosophy and usually expressed in abstract language. Most of the few writers on journalistic criticism reduce the theories, for working purposes, to two, chosen from a larger group including authoritarian, judicial, classical, historical, moral, scientific, and impressionistic.

Impressionist and Authoritarian

The simplest division is into *impressionistic* and *authoritative,* for the latter embraces judicial, moral, historical, classical, and scientific.

The impressionistic critic follows the philosophy, often quoted, as set forth by Anatole France in *Our Lady's Juggler:* "The good critic is he who narrates the adventures of his soul among masterpieces." It follows logically that an ignorant, narrow-minded critic is unlikely to produce great criticism, for his thin, emaciated soul will have no adventures of consequence among masterpieces. The greater the critic, therefore, the greater the criticism. Greatness, in this context, means not only knowledge of the art before him but also tolerance, magnanimity, human understanding, and freedom from prejudice and bias.

The impressionistic critic adds something from inside himself to the reporting. He emphasizes his own impressions, rather than the facts or simple description. Such a critic does not judge a work of art on how nearly it approaches the qualities or characteristics of an earlier work; he judges it on its own merits and on its effect upon him.

The authoritarian critic, on the other hand, believes that there exist fixed standards with which to judge a new book, painting, or some other composition or performance. The authoritarian critic of a new novel by Hemingway, for instance, judges it in comparison with the previous novels by him and with other novels with the same setting or purpose. He is likely to judge a motion picture whose plot was suggested by a novel by comparing the picture with the novel; similarly, he judges a television play against the background of the legitimate theater form of that play, and vice versa. Therefore a modern novelist who violates what the critic believes to be the rules of novel writing is condemned.

Thoroughly authoritarian criticism can be produced only after years of study and exposure to the art of the past, for it is knowledge of what has gone before that gives this critic his perspective. He desires to orient his reader; he cannot do so unless he is himself oriented. The impressionistic critic, at his best, also possesses such knowledge, but he draws upon himself rather than upon outside authorities.

Wayne Gard, in his *Book Reviewing*, uses the word *judicial* for the term *authoritarian*. "Judicial criticism," he explains, "usually consists in judging a particular work by historical models which already have been accepted as good. At its worst, it seeks to inflict upon all writers the strict observance of arbitrary rules. Thus Horace required that playwrights should never have more than three actors on the stage at one time, and that all plays should have five acts. . . ." He notes that this philosophy also has been called *classical* or *moral* and that the method is being abandoned because so much material being produced defies comparison with the classics. That observation was made three decades back and now is more nearly true.

Examination of a large number of critical articles—book reviews, criticism of the dance, music, plays, and other artistic efforts—from newspapers and magazines from many parts of this country, reveals that most criticism combines the authoritarian and impressionistic approaches, and that few are dominantly authoritarian. Young critics seem to begin as authoritarians, since that is their only point of reference, but as they develop they move into impressionism.

These distinctions, it must be remembered, are theoretical. Only writers greatly interested in critical theory for its own sake give much thought to their philosophies. In the journalistic world, especially, the critic simply performs his job. It would no more occur to him deliberately to include or omit material because it is authoritarian or impressionistic than it would to parse his sentences. He is essentially himself, a journalistic creature evolved from experience and study, writing as he thinks best and not labeling his methods. But the methods are used, nonetheless, and the new critic can benefit from understanding and using them consciously until they become a part of himself, unnoticed, yet in use.

Estimates of the Theories

The two chief approaches, impressionism and authoritarianism, have been fought over for more than a half century. The bitterest days of the fighting now are over, and, among the most influential critics, impressionism has won. Although the conflict has gone on largely among the critical writers outside journalism, it has been reflected in journalism. They were mainly engaged in teaching literature or producing critical treatments of past or present writers for book publication, but many of them also wrote for the press.

Winchester, calmer than most opponents of impressionistic criticism, said: ". . . it cannot be accounted criticism. To accept such a conception of the function of criticism is to abandon all attempt to arbitrate between differing judgments, and to give up all distinctions of better or worse in letters. It substitutes individual taste, often individual caprice, for critical principle, and leaves us without any authority or certified literary tradition, at liberty to rank the fad of the hour along with the classic of the ages.

"The truth is," he also wrote in his *Principles of Literary Criticism,* "no man's single preference can be accepted as an infallible guide."

Other writers have contended that Anatole France's definition of criticism, the acme of impressionism, cannot be used for at least two reasons. One is that a new work is not necessarily a masterpiece; in fact, there are few such, and we seem to have no reliable ones except old works. It also is said that, since the impressionistic critic has no rules, he likewise has no standards. Peyre describes the extreme of impressionism as that "which ranks works of art according to the fleeting pleasure one may receive from them."

Norman Cousins, in a *Saturday Review* editorial in 1956, pointed up the weakness of the extreme impressionist as his opponents see it. He wrote:

"Criticism is meaningless unless the yardstick of the critic is visible and respected. Whatever the license of the artist the critic is under no compulsion to judge on any basis other than what he sees. He cannot make the view of the artist his own. For he represents not the artist but a public, trained or otherwise, seeking valid appraisal. Certainly the critic is not obligated to dispense exemptions for poets who write largely for each other but who present themselves for critical approbation just the same."

The impressionist viewpoint also is considered to be weak because such a critic has no other standard than his own reactions, which in reality is no standard whatsoever or at best only one standard: the totality of his own personal aesthetic level or position.

An argument that lends strength to the opponents of impressionism is the use made of this method by journalistic critics. Having once heard that it is not necessary to cleave to historic models or standards, the journalist is likely to depend too much upon the effect upon himself of what he is viewing or hearing. In any case, this type, as generally encountered in journalism, is easily and quickly written. Because the *best* impressionist critics are possessed of eager and searching minds, good taste, and familiarity with the history of the arts, it stands to reason that it is impossible for most journalistic critics to do excellent work until they have had time to develop in themselves the qualities that result only from study of the arts and exposure to all their manifestations.

The defenders of authoritarian criticism have been far more vocal than the proponents of impressionism. Whole volumes have been thrown into the fight on the authoritarian side by W. C. Brownell, Paul Elmer More, and many others.

Having standards, in one sense, means that the critic believes in some outside rules of form for the work of art. The authoritarian critic, as we have noted, holds up a new work to such rules, like the one, for instance, that says a short story may not be a single incident but must be a series of events or incidents reaching a climax. The authoritarian critic takes over the standards of his group. These are many. They vary according to the art under examination and the work itself. Criteria applied to paintings, for instance, vary greatly from those imposed on telecasts of plays.

A clear example of standards set up for a particular art form is a set of eight rules which Edgar Dale, the Ohio State University educator, has evolved. In his book, *How to Appreciate Motion Pictures,* Dale suggested these standards, among others, for evaluating the quality of movie stories:

"1. A good motion-picture story must really do what it sets out to do.

"2. The story should be so built that there is a consistent rise in interest from the beginning of the picture until the climax."

A writer in *Cassell's Encyclopedia of World Literature* opposes such lists by declaring: "Our philosophy is what life has taught us; our principles of literature are what our literary experience has taught us. We cannot expect to establish a code of literary laws for others; we ought not to hope that others will make a code of literary laws for us. Our worth as literary critics largely depends upon our ability to free our minds from cant, obsolete psychology, unexamined contradictions, docile acceptance of fashion and insolent defiance of fashion, words masquerading as thoughts, a sense of superiority to the past and a sense of the inferiority of the present. If these are our aims, the absence of definable 'standards' (whether ethical or esthetic) becomes less disturbing."

Henri Peyre also wrote about the futility of seeking a rigid yardstick when he said, in his *Basis:* "Without delay we might then brush aside all the errors of criticism and seek an infallible basis for our future critical judgments in psychology, semantics, statistics, or some other so-called 'exact' discipline. Such a Utopian venture would soon lead to new disappointments."

But even the simpler resort to comparison with previous works of the same nature has its dangers. These were graphically explained during 1938 by an anonymous editorialist in *The Saturday Review* when he wrote: "We often read reviews submitted by young reviewers who would like to write for these columns, and we are struck by one quality common to most of them—the attempt to compare a current novel with 'War and Peace,' a current biography with Boswell or even Plutarch. The matter is certainly reduced to the absurd when a reviewer writes, for instance, in all solemnity, that a novel by Lloyd C. Douglas is not so good as a novel by Dostoevski . . . it is an extreme illustration of the fact that there are many books to which literary standards cannot appropriately be applied . . . To confine discussion of books to the analysis of their purely literary qualities will uphold not literary standards, but intellectual snobbery."

If impressionistic criticism can result in anarchy and if authoritarian too often runs to insistence upon following rigid rules, what is the journalistic critic's choice? Is there no middle ground? Certainly there is between the extremes. What is the practice of the leading journalistic critics of this day? Can they be pigeonholed? A reading of their material shows that they combine impressionism and authoritarianism, with an inclination more toward one than the other, depending upon the nature of the critic and varying by art. Impressionism at present is popular among art critics; authoritarianism among radio-television critics.

Usually, however, our leading critics are undisturbed if the rules are broken so long as the effect of such breaking upon them is to convince them that the result nevertheless is artistic. For example, see the reviews in the New York newspapers and the leading magazines of literature and the theater of any of the plays of Samuel Beckett and particularly of the dramatization of parts of James Joyce's novel, *Ulysses*, titled *Ulysses in Nighttown*.

There have been rules for the arts as well as for the art of criticism. Historians of both say that these formulae or criteria have changed from time to time, those accepted at one period being denounced in another and then restored to favor, much like an ancient emperor's mistresses. Peyre, however, says that "Criticism must always remain an adventure or an act of faith." In that case, the existence of constant rules is a defiance of freedom in the arts, and since criticism, being writing, is part of literature and therefore an art itself, it cannot be thus hidebound. To writers on criticism, like Irving Babbitt, Brownell, and many others, including a few social scientists who have taken an interest in this matter, there are specific rules. But it is difficult to understand how criticism can be organized and regimented to the point where, except for minor journalistic regulations, a formula can be worked out so that a new critic can produce a book review much as he would use a blueprint to build himself a sailboat. Even to set down a few specific tests immediately plunges him who formulates them into a debate over the very meaning of terms.

The Attitudes of the Critic

Perhaps attitudes are of more importance than rules to the journalistic critic. One of these should be open-mindedness, not to the point of vacuity but to the extent of avoiding dogmatism. Peyre recounts the closed-mindedness of many critics when the paintings of Cézanne, Gauguin, Van Gogh, Picasso, and Derain were exhibited in 1910 in London. In our time it is the work of Dali, Pollock, and some others that still is hooted at by some critics as well as most ordinary citizens, aided by journalistic feature writers who continue to make stock jokes about cows, birds, and apes that paint and are mistaken for human artists.

The value of open-mindedness, of willingness to try to understand the strange, the obscure, or the offbeat, is illustrated in reverse by Randall Jarrell, the American poet and teacher, who has reported that he read, in an issue of the London *Times* printed in 1851, a review of a new book by Alfred Tennyson. To several adversely critical sentences the reviewer added: "Another fault is not peculiar to 'In Memoriam'; it runs through all Mr. Tennyson's poetry—we allude to his obscurity."

George Jean Nathan, however, did not share the view that the critic should come to "each and every book or play with an open and unprejudiced mind." That, he said, "is to be expected only of the critical amateur and dilettante. Behind every book or play there is an author or a playwright and behind the author or playwright there is, in many instances, a record of previous performance. Where a complete lack of merit has been observable in such antecedent performances, I find myself unable to approach the new work without a certain prejudice against it. This prejudice has not turned out to be ill-founded, I have discovered, for in a quarter of a century of reviewing I have known a case where an author or a playwright already put down as talentless has suddenly and miraculously turned into a genius overnight."

And J. Donald Adams, writing in the New York *Times* many years later, agreed that scientific objectivity is undesirable. "It is possible for a generous and open-minded man to offer a friend disinterested advice on a practical problem, or to criticize impartially an act of his, but nobody can speak disinterestedly about a work of art."

To be sure, as Lowell put it, "A wise skepticism is the first attribute of a good critic," but this does not mean making no effort to push into the background prejudices which one possesses about an art or an artist. The extreme toward which failure to make this effort can go was illustrated during the Hitler regime in Germany. The late Louis P. Lochner, in his autobiography, *Always the Unexpected,* recalled that "Instead of criticism in musical and artistic matters, Goebbels ordered *Betrachtungen* (Contemplations). That meant, for instance, if a painter or a pianist was in the good graces of the party, contemplation had to be limited to a mention of the exhibit or the program and a eulogy pointing out how the artist had helped the Nazi cause." The artistic history of Russia since 1919 is another illustration of the almost total loss of an attempt at objectivity. This was dramatically highlighted by Boris Pasternak's refusal of the 1958 Nobel Prize.

Arriving at standards means making value judgments. Early critics were authoritarian, for they assumed the existence of infallible rules for a work of art. The modern critic's problem is to use standards without being dogmatic. He may wish to do what S. Stevenson Smith has suggested in his *The Craft of the Critic:* ". . . not try to estimate one work in terms of another; still less in terms of some predetermined set of formulas derived from the common characteristics of many works. This is to yield too much to a false analogy between critical method and the older scientific practice of classification."

Another attitude of the free critic is internationalism. He should not be chauvinistic, alleging that only works that uphold American or French or some other national views are to be accepted. Nor should he insist upon national subjects or settings.

A moralistic attitude is to be shunned. Peyre shows the folly of this. He cites a critic of *Jane Eyre* who said that the Brontë story had "a coarseness of language and laxity of tone which have no excuse in our time. . . ." He also notes that Hawthorne's *Scarlet Letter,* now a schoolroom classic, was denounced thus:

"Let this brokerage of lust be put down at the very beginning. Already, among the million, we have imitations enough of George Sand and Eugene Sue; and if as yet there be no reputable name involved in the manufacture of a Brothel Library, we congratulate the country that we are yet in time to save such a reputation as that of Hawthorne."[1]

All these attitudes rest on one which, while impossible to achieve perfectly, sometimes is set forth as the ideal for the journalist: the attitude of objectivity. This one, too, is debated. If the critic succeeds in achieving complete objectivity, he is no more than a writer of diagnoses, a summarizer of many viewpoints, an observer and only superficially a perfect one at that. If a function of the critic is to appreciate, to guide, to help a listener or reader or viewer to understand, he must be more than objective and must venture into the realm of opinion. If the critic is to apprehend and comprehend the truth discerned by the artist, he must use his own mind in the process. And no human is objective; each of us possesses certain prejudices and preconceptions. The criticisms we write inevitably reflect these predilections, thus absolute objectivity is an unreachable goal. The critic soon learns that his thoughtful readers have decided that it is far better to understand the critic's bent and to discount his work accordingly. If, for example, he has a known lack of sympathy for the work of Jackson Pollock or Jacob Epstein (or it is known that he is a vigorous propagandist for one of these controversial artists), his more astute readers will allow for that known inclination. The existence of critics of diverging views allows readers or listeners to make up their own minds about the degree of enjoyment of other rewards they can expect from the art under criticism.

While the critic should be open-minded in his willingness to give any work of art a fair examination, he must bring to it some background of knowledge of the artist, of his school, of the period in which he worked or works. In so doing he carries prejudices,

[1] Father Harold C. Gardiner, literary editor, *America*, has evolved "Five Principles for Moral Evaluations." As set forth in his pamphlet, *Tenets for Readers and Reviewers*, they illustrate a saner viewpoint from a moral critic of the arts.

to be sure, but they are not necessarily fixed. But they often are dogmatism.

Politics, for instance, plays a part in criticism, and can destroy objectivity and fairness of appraisal. A reviewer of a volume on politics itself certainly cannot easily separate his own views from those of the author. His opinions also enter when he examines a book of verse by a writer of distinct political opinions. The temptation of a reviewer of a new book of poems by Ezra Pound to take Pound's political position too much into consideration is great, just as it would be in writing a review of a recital by Paul Robeson. Detachment from literary or other artistic schools is equally difficult, as view the critical battles in the days of Stuart Sherman, Irving Babbitt, and Paul Elmer More. Paul Hume, the Washington music critic, learned that it took courage to be adversely critical of President Truman's daughter Margaret.

The ultimate test of a critic's ability might be made if he is denied knowledge of who wrote or drew the work of art but is expected to evaluate it on its merits. During its too-short life, *The Tiger's Eye*, an American literary magazine, followed the practice of publishing unsigned work, except that in the center were several pages containing the contents list, with the names of the artists and writers and their work.

There often is antipathy on the part of critics toward the new and the unknown. Peyre has filled half a book (*Writers and Their Critics*) with the record of critical misjudgments, some of which resulted from lack of objectivity.

What T. S. Eliot said about literary criticism in his lecture on "The Frontiers of Criticism" at the University of Minnesota in 1954 (when 13,000 persons came out to hear one of the world's most erudite and obscure or difficult poets) applies to all subjects for criticism. "If," he said, ". . . we place all the emphasis upon understanding, we are in danger of slipping from understanding to mere explanation. We are in danger of pursuing criticism as if it was a science, which it never can be. If, on the other hand, we overemphasize *enjoyment*, we will tend to fall into the subjective and impressionistic, and our enjoyment will profit us no more than mere amusement and pastime."

Where Do We Stand?

The new journalistic critic, seated in a theater waiting for the curtain to fall after the last bow of the cast, if he has been pondering the ideas in this chapter, may feel like the neophyte golfer struggling to remember the advice of the pro as he swings his driver. At first his reflections on authoritarianism versus impressionism, unattainable complete objectivity versus easily obtained prejudice and bias, and general versus specific standards and rules may stultify him. What is he to say tonight, on the way back to the office, after having seen Hume Cronyn and Jessica Tandy in two one-act plays by Sean O'Casey? Dare he point out the anachronism of the use of a shiny cigarette lighter in a play set in the Dublin of 1925? Should he point out that Angela Nightingale, the prostitute of *Bedtime Story,* was much too neatly and well dressed for the rest of the setting? Should he observe that the Irish policeman and sailor parts played by Bryan Herbert were delightfully realistic or would this be praising someone for doing the obvious, for the parts were foolproof? Do these observations not depend on acceptance of certain rules of stagecraft?

Such thoughts begin to reveal the critic to himself. If he thinks the incident of the lighter important, he has indeed selected a rule and shows he thinks it broken. If, on the other hand, he dismissed that and the other observations like it as superficial, and thinks, instead, about the total effect of the plays, noting that they illuminate life in Ireland, that they aroused certain emotions in him, and gave him understanding of the characters, his review will ignore small faults of casting or design and concentrate on these impressions. He then may help his readers to see the meaning and significance of the plays that, usually being less sensitive observers, they did not grasp. And here, again, the critic has learned something about himself. He may change himself if he wishes, but as he continues to analyze and appreciate and write he will develop his philosophy of criticism more firmly, just as he evolves his own style.

The Critic's Style

The journalistic critic's style is limited by the type of publication in which his work appears or the audience he addresses.

It might seem more reasonable to say that a critic with a clear, understandable style is qualified to appear in any publication. In general this is true; strictly speaking it is not. The critic's writing may be suitable for most publications or other media but fail for the specialized critical journal; that is, for the technically well-informed readers whom it tries to serve.

The journalistic world, hence the critical writer's market, is divided into levels which might be represented diagrammatically, in terms of population characteristics, by a rectangle lying on one side. A narrow strip at the left represents a small group of illiterates, who, nevertheless, may be appreciators of the non-written arts and have some artistic ability. To their right is a wide section representing the educationally limited portion of the population, persons with minimal ability to read but no interest in the written word, except for the most pragmatic purposes, and no knowledge of criticism or its functions. Further to the right comes the great bulk of the American population, the middle class. Their reading material is popular. For them, and their like in other countries, the world's largest magazine, *The Reader's Digest,* is published, as are other multimillion circulation books, newspapers, and periodicals. Here may be found casual interest in critical writing; such interest is nurtured by the newspaper device of using stars, asterisks, or other symbols to show critical ratings of motion pictures, television shows, and radio programs. These readers, however, have no concern for the refinements of criticism and respond to no involved analyses.

Frank E. Tripp, while chairman of the board of the Gannett group of newspapers, had a column in which he one day wrote on "Speaking of Critics." His description of the usual newspaper reader might be read profitably each day by every critic whose work appears in a publication read by the ordinary American citizen.

"A poor guy who was brought up on base hits, delayed passes, hammerlocks, uppercuts, hook balls, dribbles—and deuces wild, when he gets old—hasn't a Chinaman's chance to look wise in an art gallery, a chamber of music, or even keep awake over the book-of-the-month. That is, he hasn't if he must depend upon what the critics write.

"He's sure they are just getting even with him when he reads that a picture he liked was astringent rather than earthy; that a number through which he slept was hung upon a framework of commedia dell' arte; that the husky basso he applauded at the wrong time was a rank pinch hitter from the minors and in miserable rasping voice; that the daubs he thought a swell likeness of the old blast furnace is a modernistic allegoric portrayal of wicked man's destiny. He thought the figure in it was a puddler homeward bound with a jag."

Mr. Tripp notes also that he himself once was a sports writer whose jargon was unintelligible to all except sports fans.

We now have reached the right-hand side of the diagram. Here is a narrow area which can conveniently be labeled as that in which the intellectuals or sophisticates are found, including the writers, sculptors, architects, and other artists themselves. These readers and listeners have no patience with the simple critical essays aimed at the bulk of the populace, for such writing is considered superficial and naive. These are the readers prepared for a style comprised of specialized words and complex concepts. They demand professional and technical criticism. It is they who support the small circulation magazines of their particular interests, who start little theater groups, who insist upon showing their sculpture and paintings in the public squares. The style for them can be as technical as necessary and as replete with the jargon as the writer wishes to make it. But he cannot expect anyone outside to comprehend what he is trying to say.

This cultural division of the population is based not only on the educational background of Americans in the second half of the twentieth century but also on their ability to appreciate and

THE FOURTH ESTATE . . .   *By Trent*

"This Summer stock production shouldn't happen to a barn!"

Courtesy, *Editor & Publisher*

enjoy the arts themselves. Carl Grabo, in his book, *The Creative Critic*, sees this picture: "Popularization filters slowly from the more to the less sophisticated. This is the way of artistic expansion. The books and music which in one generation are appreciated by only the few, in the progress of time and the broadening of education become the enjoyment of the many."

The journalism of this country, if it is to survive without subsidy, must be profit-making. Its owners, especially those issuing publications (or programs) seeking mass distribution and response, beam content at the various groups and subgroups in our rectangle. It is improbable that any one critic's style will please everyone; nor is it necessary that this be the case.

Oscar Thompson, in his *Practical Musical Criticism,* observed that "The critic's writing will reflect the artist and the man. The essentials are that it be clear and that it possess reader interest. Beyond that, let the reviewer fulfil his obligations to himself, his employers and the art . . . He will write well if he can. And he will write his own way."

This counsel is sound, provided it be understood that "clear" is a relative word, for what is clear to a reader with a given background and knowledge of words may not be to another who brings different equipment to his reading of a critical article or a review.

The chief portion of the total audience that the American critic of the arts can hope to reach is the middle class. Readers and audiences are more numerous there than in the narrow section to the right of the diagram whose inhabitants we generally call the intellectuals. And, being more numerous, more publications, performances, and programs are intended for them. Among the middle class the critic can find a variety of interests in critical writing that is, however, dominantly superficial. The criticism serves too often as a substitute for what is criticized, much as digest versions of articles and books are accepted in place of the full-length version.

Our analysis of the population is subject to modification according to whether the middle class is determined on an economic or an educational rating. A number of economically middle-class people, drawn from such professions as the ministry, law, medicine, and teaching, are interested in reviews and criticisms that are thorough and penetrating.

Martin Mayer calls the writing for the middle class "service criticism" because it is a manifestation of surface democracy. This manifestation gives the reviewer the idea that his obligation is to the reader rather than to the art itself. The service critic's style, therefore, is bound to be easy for anyone to understand.

Journalistic Style

Except when writing for erudite and specialized journals, journalistic critics conform to the stylistic traditions of the press; critics who depend upon the spoken word similarly adjust to the level of their medium. If they do not, they no longer are read or heard. Journalistic style is characterized by use of short sentences; simple words; brief paragraphs; avoidance of foreign terms and exotic references and, except where inescapable, of technical art terms; brightness and newsiness of tone; and introduction of human interest wherever possible. Journalistic writing in the United States is plain, inclined to dependence upon the cliché, repetitious (it is charged with telling its story thrice: in headline, opening paragraph, and body of the account), and selective of the trivial rather than the important.

To what extent does journalistic criticism follow the rules of the newspaper or wire service newsroom or the magazine editorial office? The critic shares the editorial and article writers' measure of freedom, although not so much as the sports writer or as little as the police or city hall reporter. The critic, since he is thought to appeal to a somewhat better-educated group of readers, is allowed to use a few of the technical words of his occupation and the specialized language of the art he is evaluating. It may appear cynical, but it is true to say that on many a publication his copy is scarcely read before publication and is ignored in print by most of the staff unless he offends some local artist or the supporters of some artistic group, with resulting angry complaints.

By and large, however, the bulk of the critical writing on newspapers is likely to be only a little less commonplace than other copy, for most of it is—and must be—hastily produced. Stanley Meisler, in his survey of critics on metropolitan dailies, concluded that "Few critics concern themselves with the art of writing and criticism . . . Style is not important . . . In general, there may be a wide difference between one critic and another in judgment but the writing is often equally undistinguished." Magazine critics, as is true with most magazine writers, at least of nonfiction, have the time to be more careful.

One speculates about the effect upon the styles of Edmund Wilson, Winthrop Sargeant, Harold Clurman, Irving Kolodin, Clifton Fadiman, and other magazine critics if they were expected to write their reviews in forty-five minutes, without time for revision. Magazine critics write longer material, employ a more artistic and ornate style (but not necessarily at the sacrifice of clarity), and are more detailed and thorough in their analyses, shying away less from technical jargon than do newspaper critics.

Developing a Style

A writer dumped suddenly into critical responsibilities necessarily writes in the style he possesses at the moment. If he is on a newspaper, where unexpected chucking into the job is most likely to occur, he writes his criticisms more or less in the style of the news and feature stories he has been turning out. If he is a music teacher or some other nonprofessional journalist, there is no telling how he will express himself. He, as well as the writer studying to be a critic, needs to consider what is involved in developing a style.

The sincere seeker after a useful and effective style will find many hours of helpful reading in writings on the subject by Read, Middleton Murry, Stevenson, Franklin, Schopenhauer, Quiller-Couch, Percy Marks, Maugham, Vera Brittain, and later writers. The author of *Kidnapped* is famous for his advice about imitating the styles of authors as a means of developing one's own. Shaw, in his *Advice to a Young Critic*, told him to "write a thousand words a day for the next five years for at least nine months every year." He emphasized this by going on to say: "The one certain thing is that you must write, write, write every day for several years if you are to become a master workman in your profession." Certainly a part of the master workman's kit is his style.

But Dr. Johnson was against the method of consciously developing a style: "He that has once studiously formed a style, rarely writes afterwards with complete ease." Nor did Samuel Butler approve. "Men like Newman and R. L. Stevenson seem to have taken pains," he wrote, "to acquire what they called a style as a preliminary measure—as something that they had to form before their writings could be of any value. I should like to put it on record that I never took the smallest pains with my style, have never thought about it, and do not know or want to know whether it is style at all or whether any man can take thought for his style without loss to himself and his readers."

Most writers on style, however, agree that it can and should be acquired if it does not come naturally. Vera Brittain, in her *On Being an Author,* declares that "While style must be learnt, it cannot be taught." She finds it to be a personal characteristic. "The reading of master writers cannot be undertaken too often," she then writes. "If your style is colourless and anemic, or you tend to over-polish and over-cherish a small output, you will benefit from the rich robustness of Ernest Hemingway . . . If you run to turgid verbosity, you will be helped by the deceptively simple lucidity of Jane Austen, Guy de Maupassant and Somerset Maugham. . . ."

Typical advice from a writing teacher is that of John C. French in his book, *Writing,* when he declares point-blank: "Improvement in style depends on two things—practice and self-criticism." A famous bit of counsel from Sam Johnson belongs here, to show the limits of self-criticism: "Read over your compositions, and when you meet with a passage which you think is particularly fine, strike it out." Quiller-Couch put it more bluntly: "Murder your darlings." This advice might be repeated by virtually every newspaper copy editor in the land, and many is the critic who agrees that deskmen are indeed murderers.

Whether he improves his style by borrowing the characteristics of others or by continuing to write as his personality dictates, the journalistic critic must arrive at the objective expressed by Maugham in *The Summing Up:* "A good style should show no sign of effort."

The Forms of Discourse

In the process of increasing the attractiveness of their writing in both form and style, critics may obtain help through understanding of the forms of discourse; i.e., description, exposition, argumentation, and narration. These academic distinctions (well explained in books by Marjorie H. Nicholson, Mary Ellen Chase, Frances K. Del Plaine, Lawrence H. Conrad, Paul M. Landis, and Kenneth W. Houp) should be considered resources. S. Stevenson Smith, for example, says: "There is no better way to marshal reasons for a critical position than the method of argument." He points to Shaw's style as a supreme example, for "It is rapid, spare, stripped for action like a boxer . . . Is there any style equal to Shaw's for controversy?" And as for the uses of narrative, Smith declares that "Certainly the critic needs to cultivate a turn for story-telling. He will do well to study the methods of the short story. He can use them for casting into form his revealing anecdotes, and no less in the body of the review, if he is concerned with the novel."

The Tone of Criticism

Not a few writers on style say that the writer's style relates to the writer's personality. Percy Marks, the novelist, in his *The Craft of Writing* (one of the wisest volumes on the subject), said that "Style refers to the method, the manner, and the personality of the writer. It is possible to analyze methods, to describe a manner, but the personality is as elusive as it is real and important. If we could define personality, we could define style. . . ."

He added that "the style of the writing should reflect the personality of the writer," and that when "a student has learned to give a true expression of himself he has achieved style." The reader will find it worth the trouble to search out Marks' application of this to the writing of Theodore Dreiser, too elaborate to be included here.

The tone of criticism has various characteristics, resulting from the nature of the writer. These include ornateness, simplicity, smartness, preciousness, banality, pomposity, humorousness, to name a few that will be considered in this chapter. That personality can transfer these to writing is illustrated by the late George Jean Nathan. The drama critic was an iconoclast, as was his long-time editorial colleague, H. L. Mencken. In his *Testament of a Critic*, Nathan not only reveals this characteristic but also explains a type of critical-writing style: the critical dodge. He wrote: "In much the same category as our young so-called radical playwrights who attempt to conceal the fact that they have nothing to say by saying it in a new and alarming manner, fall certain of our critics who, also having nothing new to say, attempt to conceal the fact by saying it in that quiet, précieuse, old-fashioned manner that passes in certain quarters for dignity of mind and solidity of judgment."

Humor, always difficult to write, has a small place in American journalistic criticism, provided now and then by *The New Yorker, Time,* and a few other periodicals and a newspaper writer here and there. Much of the drabness of newspaper and magazine criticism could be relieved if there were more passages like:

"Esther Williams' pictures are generally just so much water over the dame," which appeared in *Time,* also the source for: "Odets, where is thy sting?" in commenting on the playwright's first movie.

". . . she played it like Whistler's Mother on a spree" was the verdict of an unidentified Toledo newspaper critic on Julie Haydon's portrayal of a prostitute in *The Time of Your Life.*

When Dorothy Parker was writing drama reviews for *Vanity Fair,* she said of a play called *The House Beautiful:* " 'The House Beautiful' is the play lousy." And, as Shaw once quipped: "A dramatic critic is a man who leaves no turn unstoned."

"Miss Loren may be the Body Beautiful," wrote Anne Marie Duval in the Schenectady *Union-Star,* "but she also is the Face Stone. Given a trying role, she comes equipped with three standard expressions—kittenish, grieved, and impassive—mostly impassive."

As Frederic Birmingham has said: "Of course, it must be confessed that we are all fond of the vitriolic critic. We like the snarl in the balcony, the asp in the honey." But wisecracking and punning can, of course, be overdone. Billy Wilder, in a letter to *Time,* went it one better on this score when he said: ". . . I find myself increasingly nauseated by the 21-pun salute which greets each new picture . . . Why doesn't he [the critic] take on somebody his own size . . . I suggest a sunrise duel—with puns at 20 paces. And may the best man wince."

The difference between humor and show-offism is a matter of taste, an undefinable quality. The writer might test himself by asking if he is using an expression because it says what he means or because it makes him look bright and clever. He also should consider at whom his barbs are directed. An arrived professional can take it, but a new artist should not be taunted for the sake of smart rhetoric. Every critic might well ask himself, before he turns his copy over to an editor: "Would I want this said of me?"

Related to humor, because above or below the level of ordinary writing, are pomposity, preciousness, ornamentation of style, and excessive resort to technical jargon. A typical piece of chesty writing from one of the literary quarterlies is:

"Patterns of imagery, on the other hand, or fragments of significance, are oracular in origin, and derive from the epiphanic moment, the flash of instantaneous comprehension with no direct reference to time, the importance of which is indicated by Cassirer in *Myth and Language.*"

Or this snobbery:

"With the Philharmonic and the Metropolitan Company both away on tour, the flow of major musical doings dwindled sharply last week, and the situation caused me to attend a couple of events that I would not ordinarily have covered." This critic's descent into the slums was to see a revival of *The Merry Widow* and to hear a performance of the oratorio, *King David.*

But it is not necessary to go to the magazines for sophisticates to find such examples. From a Washington daily comes this pompous bit: "Palmer's sonata finds him at his best, as in his piano quartet. Solid, built of rhythmic intricacies that provide a massive effect without heaviness, and achieving a cumulative effect through dissonant polyphony that uses the piano with enormous power and skill, the piece has a highly personal beauty and effect."

Llewellyn Jones, in his *How to Criticize Books,* tells of the occasion when he learned the word " 'xenophobia' . . . just a day or so before writing a review of a book about the restriction of immigration and the persecution of aliens," and thought it a piece of luck that at first seemed good. He goes on to say, however, ". . . having just learned the word, I had to use it in the heading I wrote for that review—and it may have scared away a number of readers."

The Toronto newspaper music critic who wrote ". . . we were impressed by her ability to establish a rhythmic quality and to draw out diminuendi and crescendi with equal subtlety," might take seriously Jones' further observation that ". . . even more bad writing is due to the fact that the writer is using words—not ideas or pictures."

And since this passage is from music criticism, an observation by Oscar Thompson in his *Practical Musical Criticism* might be pondered by such a critic: ". . . the taste with which he expresses himself, whether in the simplest terms or the most erudite, is a fair measure of the taste with which he listens to music."

The Critic's Clichés

But by far the greater fault in journalistic critical style is not rococo or ornamental writing, but the appallingly stale expression. Almost any general newspaper or magazine provides examples instantly. Such as:

deep resonant voice	won immediate favor
proved a serviceable Nanki-Poo	the sheer beauty of
reeled off	the lilting phrases
real box-office appeal	a stark realism
characters live in this book	the novel at its best
facile, sharply etched style	gay story
gone to great lengths to	sets are well done
skillful characterization	a continuous flow of laughter
rare ability	perfect timing

Such triteness and banality result primarily from the pace of journalism and the writers' barren vocabularies. Peyre calls it "mental inertia." One may expect students to exhibit this failing, but to find most journalistic critical writing overlaid with these stereotypes indicates a national critical writing problem.

After all, it is possible to be simple and direct without being commonplace in style. How a few words can say much is illustrated in Tom F. Driver's review of Federico Garcia Lorca's play,

Blood Wedding, when it was given at the Actor's Playhouse in New York. Writing in *The Christian Century,* for which he is drama critic, he said, albeit somewhat ungrammatically:

"An off-Broadway group is appearing in Lorca's *Blood Wedding.* Their production is long on scenery, short on acting, and incredible on all sides. Lorca writes a demanding poetry. In this case it seems the demands not only have not been met but have not even been recognized. *Blood Wedding,* yes. But surely a victim of tired blood."

Compared with wholesale resort to stock critical expressions, certain other stylistic weaknesses of journalistic critics are relatively minor. These include overquoting from the book being reviewed, paraphrasing so as to distort the original, and employing words inaccurately. But they are not mere peccadillos.

Sydney J. Harris, columnist and critic for the Chicago *Daily News,* once gave a lesson in book reviewing and perceptive reading. He received for review a volume about words. The first paragraph of the preface read:

"A statement that is often attributed to the proverbial 'man on the street' is that . . .

Harris' comment was that "man in the street" isn't proverbial, but colloquial, and also so trite that a discriminating writer should avoid it. And no genuine word lover would put it in quotation marks, for if the expression is worth using it is worth using in itself. The quotation marks merely show that the author is ashamed of having used the shopworn phrase. Such writing, Harris said, immediately notifies the professional that here is a writer who does not know his business.

This chapter may appear to have overemphasized the faults of style that the critic must avoid. Is there an ideal style? Possibly Oscar Thompson's description of that of W. J. Henderson provides a goal. He wrote of Henderson, music critic for the New York *Times* for twenty years and for the New York *Sun* for thirty-five, as well as author of various books on the art:

"He has rid writing of its last suggestions of effort, by perfecting a technique that reads as if it took care of itself. He goes straight to some issue, paragraph by paragraph, sentence by sentence, and, in the concentrated clarity of his style, word by word. There is no waste, no padding, no clutter of circuitous phrases. He says precisely what he wishes to say, no more, no less. Yet is he never curt, never spare. The amplitude of his ideas prevents that. His is a style as mellow and easy as it is precise and clear. The sentence structure, with each sentence a complete idea in itself, yet clearly related to what precedes and follows, explains much of this. But at the bottom of all is the word . . . none has had a happier faculty for finding the exact and illuminative term."

Samples of the Hendersonian style, of which too few have been preserved, may be found in *The Flagstad Manuscript,* which preserves the reactions to the soprano not only by Henderson but also by other notable critics, including Olin Downes, Lawrence Gilman, Samuel Chotzinoff, Pitts Sanborn, Winthrop Sargeant, Virgil Thomson, William Mann, and Oscar Thompson himself.

"Her clear enunciation," wrote Henderson about Flagstad's part in *Die Walküre,* "added to the excellence of her delivery. This was a very musical Brünnhilde, and in moments it was eloquent. But that it was tentative in some places was unquestionable . . . The outstanding features of the impersonation yesterday were the vocal splendor, the appearance of youth, and the communication of the gentler emotions."

Writing Reviews

Cyril Beaumont, a respected English critic of the ballet, wrote each of his reviews in about the same way. Richard Buckle, in his *The Adventures of a Ballet Critic,* has described in detail how Beaumont built them.

First he recapitulates the story, and lists the "previous productions of the same ballet or ballets on a similar theme; then he describes the performance in detail, giving if possible an idea of the scenery's structure and of the colours of the costumes; finally he places the production in his mind alongside some masterpiece and measures it, recording it and where it moved him emotionally, and if not, why it fell short."

Buckle calls it "this extremely logical method," and says it "can seem almost too exhaustive. . . ." It also may be wooden and far too long except for the most devoted *aficionados.* Buckle goes on to explain why he thinks this method suitable, by saying that Beaumont wrote deliberately to be helpful "to dancers and producers in a hundred or five hundred years' time. It strikes him as a tragedy that there are no full and detailed accounts of the ballets of Noverre, Perrot, and Petipa as they were first produced, and he does not intend this grave omission to apply to our century."

Such extensive criticism is most suitable for magazines or books; in fact, much of Beaumont's work appears in his books on ballet.

His is one of the two common ways to construct a review.[1]

[1] To avoid confusion, this chapter will use the word *review* to designate a short piece of critical writing, as for a newspaper or magazine, about a particular art event, to distinguish it from the full-length criticism known as the critical article, which is dealt with in the next chapter.

The other method is that of the writer who follows no regular pattern. One such is John Martin, dance critic of the New York *Times*, who usually emphasizes, in his opening paragraphs, the journalistic five W's before settling down to criticize. His is largely an impressionistic review from there on, with no particular formula for the analysis; that is, he does not regularly take up the choreography first, say, and then the performances of individuals. Journalistic critics in the matter of literary structure, then, are like other writers of journalism. They fall into two main groupings: those who, like Beaumont, follow a more or less fixed pattern and those, like Martin, who vary the architecture of their writing. This is not to say, however, that a majority follow Beaumont's scheme. On the contrary; there is considerable diversity in form.

Diversity Is the Rule

Many generalizations have been made about American journalistic criticism, in this book and elsewhere, but there is one that cannot be made: that the writing is uniform. Precisely because so many of the writers are journalists they give their reviews and articles variety of form and content.

The literal review, that is, the reportorial piece entirely devoid of criticism, as we have seen in Chapter 1, is uncommon. When it does occur (and it might well be used in place of the inadequate criticisms ventured by new writers), it is likely to follow the traditional pattern of news writing in the United States. It has a lead, or summary opening section, followed by the unfolding of details of decreasing order of importance.

No accepted pattern of any sort exists for writing reviews. Although much of the writing may be mediocre and the insights frequently shallow, there is an astonishing variety in the way journalistic critics build their reviews. Patterns are far more often discernible in the full-length critical article (*see* Chapter 9), but an attempt to find any important uniformity in reviews is fruitless.

It is possible to record here a few more often used ways to begin or end reviews, but they lack the complexity of ways to construct news and feature stories. News stories, for example, have as many as forty distinct formulas for opening sections, built on grammatical and rhetorical forms, with names such as cartridge lead and the participial lead.

But critical writing, being almost always signed, encourages the writer to individuality of expression. Patterns in journalism were invented so reporters could write more quickly; they are especially helpful to journalists seated at typewriters in city rooms who must get the news over the radio or telephone. The critic usually has a little more time than the beat reporter and the rewrite man (the reviewer of a first-night show may be the exception), and certainly the magazine critic has no excuse for slapping his material into a mold.

What are some of the ways used by critics in developing their reviews? Here are some of the many: constructing the review around personal experience, such as recalling an encounter with the star of the performance; dispensing first with the new aspects and then venting their opinions; launching a generalization about the event and then backing it up with evidence; relating an anecdote or reporting an incident which leads into the opinions to be presented.

Departures from the straight essay form for the review are scarce, especially in newspapers. It takes considerable time and staying power to vary from the conventional essay form of the usual review. Bosley Crowther, movie critic of the New York *Times*, reviewed *Jubal* entirely in verse, turning out a 52-line criticism which began:

> "Won't you slip into my bedroom?"
> Coos the fat ranch-owner's wife
> To the ambulating cowboy
> Who has come into her life.

Charles Poore, one of that same paper's staff of book reviewers, dealt with *The Diaries of Lewis Carroll* by writing his entire review in the manner of *Alice in Wonderland*. His colleague, Orville Prescott, handled Phyllis McGinley's *Love Letters* by writing her a letter (". . . and I feel that I must write you a love letter right now"). Herbert Mitgang, also a *Times* man, handled *Happy New Year, Kamerades!* by Robert J. C. Lowry, by writing a dialogue between The Reader and The Writer. Other devices have been the diary form and imitation of the style of the artist.

Constructing the Review

Reviewing can be reduced to a formula. Although to be shunned by the experienced professional, it is of considerable help to the floundering beginner if he learns eventually to dispense with the pattern. Depending upon his purpose, the reviewer may deliberately devote certain amounts of space to particular types of content. Here are several workable formulas:

1 part strict review (the five W's),
2 parts recapitulation of plot or action or description of appearance,
5 parts criticism, either all authoritative or all impressionistic or a combination.

1 part review,
1 part criticism of either or both types,
1 part recapitulation.

1 part review,
1 part criticism.

What determines the proportions of straight reporting and evaluation may be what the writer thinks the reader or listener can absorb or what space or time he has available for presenting the material. The less experienced the reviewer the safer it is to emphasize the reporting over the criticism, whether the latter be favorable or unfavorable.

Commonly, critics give about half of their space to recapitulation of plot (as with novels, dancing, movies, and plays), and divide the rest between the five W's and their views. What is pragmatically successful can be gauged by studying the reviews of effective critics, *effective* here meaning not only those with a wide following but also those who influence the art they criticize.

Constructing a review is a process of selecting material. A century ago it was common for a critic, particularly of literature, to devote two or three thousand words to his review of one book. Except in scholarly journals and the lead reviews of a book section or literary magazine, this rarely occurs today. The journalistic critic determines what he shall include by deciding what he wants to say about the art, thinking of what his readers may require of him and "keeping it short." If, with the egotism a critic must possess to transcend simple journalism, he emphasizes his reactions he may lose certain readers; but, if he writes simply to gratify his readers, he may develop a commonplace article that loses him certain others. After all, many a reader of criticism merely wants to know "what the critic thought of it" (note the practice of *Newsweek* in summarizing its critics' opinions with a one-line conclusion at the end of each review), and may have little interest in the reviewer's reasons for arriving at his conclusions. Such readers have a dangerous influence on the critic; they make him think that his reasoning is unimportant, whereas it may be his true contribution to journalism.

Beginning, Middle, Ending

* Many journalists, even some of the most experienced, ought to consider automatically throwing out the opening paragraph or two of what they have written, for often it is little more than a wordy winding up or a set of dubious generalizations. If one risks doing this it is surprising to find that what one has to say actually begins with the third paragraph. The reviewer who does not think out his opening is likely to overwrite.

The middle section might appear to be the most important part of the essay, but it is not so for the average reader, even though it may contain the heart of the reviewer's views. It should be constructed, nevertheless, to carry the essential summaries and opinions but be brisk and concise, so as not to lose the impatient skimmer.

The ending, thought by some journalists to be the second most important part of the review after the opening paragraph, is almost as difficult to construct as the beginning. There is danger that it may taper off into vapidity or into sweeping statements that have not properly been led up to. Several sound possibilities exist, as the practices of major reviewers illustrate, among them being: (1) a summation of the critic's main points; (2) a major point that is an integral part of the body of the article.

A sound rule that will help the writer avoid pontification and dubious generalizations is generally to write only about the recital, book, building, or whatever he is reviewing and avoid using it as an excuse to roam over the field, develop a trend, discuss a group of artists, or deal with some other topic that serves mainly as background. There should be adventures into these by-passes, but they should be rare.

Preparation of Copy

From the basis for selection of content to the preparation of copy is a descent into a highly practical matter, but the trip must be made. In the realm of critical writing, instructions for copy preparation include more than the usual ones about proper spacing and placement of copy upon the page. Since the details of these rules are available in standard texts (Berry's *Journalism Today*, Wolseley's and Campbell's *Exploring Journalism*, or Mott's *New Survey of Journalism*), they will not be repeated here.

One aspect of such copy preparation, however, is peculiar to critical writing that is to appear in print: the presentation of the indicia or summary material that precedes a review. There are minor variations in content and typography that the writer can learn by studying the practice of the publication for which he is writing. (See p. 105.)

No particular form is used for the arts other than those shown in the reproductions. Many writers avoid these convenient summaries altogether and weave these basic facts into their reviews, perhaps because preparing such a summary, particularly for a play or opera with a large cast, is a routine chore. Sometimes the integrated facts are high-lighted in the criticism by being bold-faced or italicized.

TYPICAL SUMMARIES TO PRECEDE REVIEWS

BOOKS

TESTAMENT OF EXPERIENCE by Vera Brittain. Macmillan, 1957. 480 pp., $5.

RECORDINGS

FRANCESCATTI PLAYS KREISLER: Zino Francescatti, violinist, Artur Balsam, pianist. Columbia Records, ML 5255.

MOTION PICTURES

LA LUPA (The She Wolf), screen play by Alberto Lattuada, Luigi Malerba, Alberto Moravia and Antonio Pietrangeli; directed by Signor Lattuada. A Ponti De Laurentiis Production released here by Jules Levey. At the World.

La Lupa	Kerima
Nanni Lasca	Ettore Manni
Maricchia	May Britt
Imborbone	Mario Passante
Young Girl	Maresa Gallo

MUSIC (CONCERT & OPERA)

BOSTON SYMPHONY ORCHESTRA, Charles Munch conducting. At Carnegie Hall.

Overture to Das Christelflein	Pfitzner
Symphony No. 4	Schumann
Fantaisies Symphoniques (Symphony No. 6)	Martinu
Symphony No. 2	Brahms

PLAYS

AMBASSADOR THEATER

A revival of the play in two acts and six scenes by Bernard Shaw, adapted by Arnold Moss, staged by Margaret Webster, settings and lighting by Marvin Reiss, costumes by Patricia Zipprodt, presented by The Theater Guild in association with Mr. Moss with the following cast: Tyrone Power, Faye Emerson, Arthur Treacher, Valerie Bettis, Arnold Moss and Richard Easton.

METROPOLITAN OPERA HOUSE

Opera in four acts, libretto by Lorenzo da Ponte, music by Wolfgang Amadeus Mozart. The cast:

Count Almaviva	George London
Countess Almaviva	Lucine Amara
Susanna	Dolores Wilson
Figaro	Giorgio Tozzi
Cherubino	Rosalind Elias
Marcellina	Margaret Roggero
Don Bartolo	Ezio Flagello
Don Basilio	Alessio De Paolis
Don Curzio	Gabor Carelli
Antonio	Lorenzo Alvary
Barbarina	Mildred Allen

Two Peasant Girls

Madeleine Chambers; Helen Vanni Conductor, Erich Leinsdorf; stage director, Hans Busch; sets designed by Jonel Jorgulesco; costumes by Ladislas Czettel; choreography by Zachary Solov.

The Legal Angles

No writer can safely be ignorant of the laws of journalism that cover libel and slander, plagiarism, copyright, and related topics. Ample counsel can be found in basic books on law of the press and literature by Thayer, Siebert, Arthur, Crosman, Wittenberg, and Steigleman. Knowledge of these matters has particular pertinency for critics, since they express opinions, and opinions are the commonest source of libel and slander. The critic is at liberty to say what he wishes about the work of art itself, but must be careful not to reflect upon the artist in a way that damages him professionally.

Other Mechanics

A common question raised by a new critic is: "How long shall I make my review?" There is no single answer. The practice of American journalism with all copy is to "keep it short," a favorite city room injunction. But what is meant by *short?* Reviews of any of the art forms may run from a few sentences to several thousand words. Length usually is determined by the medium. The new reviewer who wishes to get practice writing can select a publication as a model and imitate its length policies. In general, it may be said that newspaper copy runs shorter than magazine material, that ordinary newspaper criticisms of plays, music, books, painting, sculpture, and radio-television run from 300 to 600 words in length.

Also raised, particularly by book reviewers, is the question: "How much shall I quote?" Books, especially of fiction, often contain, on the copyright page, some such stricture as this: "All rights reserved. No part of this book may be reproduced in any form without the permission of [the publisher]." Others say: "No part in excess of 500 words . . ." or some other figure. Still others consider the reviewer directly and insert some such clause as "except in the case of brief quotations embodied in critical articles and reviews." How long is *brief?* As a rule of thumb, at this writing 300 words or no more than 1 per cent of the total wordage, whichever is less, in the source is considered permissible.

Quotations from the original should be included, for they give the reader a clue to the author's style and lend authenticity to the review. But they should be brief, certainly not occupying more than 5 to 10 per cent of the total review. And quoted passages should not be lumped or grouped, for unless they consist of narrative they are not of great interest to the reader of general newspapers or magazines. It is better to alternate direct and indirect quotations; even typographically this is more desirable than long stretches of quoted matter.

Note-taking is a technique worth considerable attention and is fundamental to the success of the new critic. Unless the writer has a most retentive memory, he is wise to make notes while listening to a concert or seeing a play or wandering about an art gallery. When reviewing a book, he will find it helpful not only to underscore passages for comment or quotation but also to note on the flyleaf his observations, with page numbers keyed to them, or to indicate his reactions on the book's margins. Such notes should be made in complete sentences and with all words, especially names, dates, and titles not in the volume itself, spelled out, for when these scribbles are cold they may not be easily readable, especially if prepared in a dubious shorthand system of one's own invention.

Producing the Review

Long-experienced critics begin framing their reviews while seeing or hearing what they are to criticize: opening paragraphs sometimes occur to them effortlessly. On the way to the writing or speaking place—home, studio, office—the body of the review may take shape also, so that by the time the critic is seated to do his writing he has well in mind what he wishes to say. Some critics make no advance plans, but work out the scheme, if any, immediately before starting to compose; others begin at a convenient point and let the association of ideas carry them along. How one produces his review is a personal matter. Obviously, if the results obtained are jumbled, the method in use is suspect and some other should be tried. Lucky is the reviewer with a wise editor who guides him in such matters.

Robert C. Marsh, music critic for the Chicago *Sun-Times*, sent the author a helpful description of his method. "I have my lead all worked out before the end of the concert (sometimes something happens at the last that makes me revise it), and a pretty clear idea of the points to be taken up and the order in which they are to be raised," he wrote. "If I know how much space I am going to have, I may actually try to think it through in exact detail, otherwise I'll give myself some options to allow for cuts I may have to make. If I walk to the office, it takes perhaps 15 minutes, I'll have the structure of the piece complete before I arrive. I'll get some coffee, check my space, and start to write. Usually I'll write the review right off, edit it very slightly, and be ready to go in a few minutes. I am often out of the office in 45 minutes (counting coffee and all). Most of my pieces are printed with very few, if any, changes, and 90% of those are simply to adjust the length by a line or so."

The trick, which Mr. Marsh says he learned in college teaching and radio work, is to think in sentences rather than phrases. The second part, he says, is to learn how to hold on to sentences once one has thought of them. "I have always found," he says, "that when I made notes I had to write them in a fashion I could read again, file them (or simply hold on to them) . . . while things I had in my head I wasn't likely to lose. Therefore a few jottings are all I will ever make—single words, spellings of names, and these have always been enough, loss proof, and reliable."

Problems and Techniques

The remainder of this chapter will consist of noting a few major problems and special techniques of reviewing the eleven different art forms covered by this book, with inclusion of a few examples as illustrations.[2]

Thorough analysis of every form would call for a book on each (and as the bibliography shows, several already have mer-

[2] In a book this size it is impossible to include examples covering all the arts and the different approaches used by journalistic critics; the reader must consult the best newspapers and magazines, often called the living textbooks of journalism.

ited book-length treatment). It is a temptation to cite only the reviews of leading critics, but these are easily available in their publications. Instead the author is deliberately quoting mostly reviews by less widely known but still competent writers, as a means of encouraging newcomers to journalistic critical writing.

ARCHITECTURE

Certainly the least evaluated of all the arts, at least by journalistic critics—what little appears is printed in specialized magazines of the profession. Although about 45 billion dollars is spent annually in this country alone on construction, general publications rarely venture into criticism of the architecture of these buildings, primarily because there is no tradition of regular architectural comment and because capable critics are not easy to come by. One consumer magazine, *The New Yorker,* has published such material occasionally by Lewis Mumford, but these are full-length articles and not reviews in the usual sense. The newsmagazines also attempt it now and then. Substantial critical articles are to be found in *Art News, Architectural Record, Architectural Forum,* and like periodicals.

BOOKS

Only the practiced reviewer can deal adequately with a book without reading it entirely. The reviewer might put himself in the position of the author and ask whether he would want his book criticized on less than a complete reading. If a reviewer can glean what is on a page quickly, he is fortunate. But skipping from haste or boredom is an injustice to the author. Skimming is more reasonable with a novel, for story and style are quickly discernible. But poetry and short stories, which may be uneven in quality and different in subject, should be read carefully. Much, as Arnold Bennett noted in his *The Truth About an Author,* is conveyed to a reviewer by the title page, author's name, the author's pedigree, the publisher's name, and the chapter headings. On these and other points writers might well consult Susan Wilbur's "Some Don'ts for Reviewers" in her husband's book, *How to Criticize Books* by Llewellyn Jones.

Reviewers of novels, plays, and movies should beware of telling the story of the entire plot. The main reason is that they cannot do justice to the work by summarizing its plot. The author's skill in creating an illusion or atmosphere is overlooked. Because he is a creative writer, he makes the unbelievable become believable, which few reviewers can do.

Critics of fact books, especially of texts, sometimes forget to show the reader the scope of the volume. While the writer need not copy the contents page wholesale, he should draw upon it as a means of showing his readers the area covered.

Reviewers of books, more so than of any other art, should remember that they may be quoted in publishers' advertising, in blurbs, and in connection with the author's next volume. Next subject to such quotation are movie and theater reviewers. The copy should be reread with this possibility in mind, not to be sure one is quotable but to be certain that quotations, when taken out of context, do not do harm. The effect upon an author of such citing is important, for talent may be squelched by needless sarcasm or unduly encouraged by sugary praises.

A Review

"Please Don't Eat the Daisies," by Jean Kerr, 187 pages, Illustrated by Carl Rose, Doubleday & Co., Inc., Garden City, N.Y.

1 For this reader's money, the 2 first and 13th articles in this book 3 are well worth its cost—some of 4 the remaining 13 fall short—per- 5 haps by comparison.

6 This, perhaps, is because this 7 reader is more familiar with the 8 unexpected situations in which a 9 parent is found when dealing with 10 children, and less acquainted with 11 Mrs. Kerr's other themes as, for 12 example, Greenwich Village.

13 But, as said above, the hilari- 14 ous chapters on how Mrs. Kerr 15 copes (there is room for consid- 16 erable doubt on how well she 17 copes) with her offspring, are 18 enough in themselves. These 19 youngsters she describes as Chris- 20 topher, "a slightly used 8-year- 21 old," Colin and Johnny, the 4- 22 year-old twins who are "dissimi- 23 lar," and Gilbert, aged 17 months.

24 Mrs. Kerr introduces the reader 25 to the four with the statement 26 that "they'll never have to pay 27 a psychiatrist $25 an hour to find 28 out why we rejected them. We'll 29 tell them why we rejected them. 30 Because they're impossible, that's 31 why."

32–37 (*Here follow the titles of a few more of the chapters, with praise for them.*)

38 As for us, we like Mrs. Kerr

39 better when she's more of a
40 homebody. Writing about her
41 children she seems less tensely
42 determined to be amusing and
43 more warmly human, therefore
44 more real to the reader.
— Ruth E. Riley, in the
Kansas City (Kans.) *Kansan*

Analysis of the Review

The reviewer begins immediately at her own interest and reason for reading the book, but she also signals, in lines 4, 8, 9, 41, and 42, that this book is not a total bargain.

The second and third paragraphs give a taste of the book's style and tone. The one thereafter (not quoted) shows the book's scope. The final paragraph contains impressionistic criticism. In general the review has taken its tone from that of the book; the reviewer also uses brief quotations effectively.

THE DANCE

Reviewers of the dance deal usually with the performances of ballet companies or recitals by individual dancers of note, supported by groups of dancers (Jose Greco, Martha Graham, Katherine Dunham).

Knowledge of the techniques is absolute as a requirement for a competent reviewer. Most persons, not having studied or practiced other than ballroom or folk dancing, simply see people hopping about a stage when they go to the ballet. The reviewer must remember this unfamiliarity and use technical jargon sparingly and, even when doing so, add an explanation.

A Review

By Manus Sasonkin

1 For its second Kiel Auditorium
2 program, the American Ballet
3 Theatre yesterday afternoon of-
4 fered four representative works:
5 "Les Patineurs," "Billy the Kid,"
6 the Grand Pas de Deux from
7 "The Nutcracker," and "Gradua-
8 tion Ball."
9 While the quality of the entire
10 program was uniformly high, I
11 felt the most intemperate enthu-
12 siasm for "Les Patineurs" from
13 "Graduation Ball," both of which
14 struck me as extraordinarily
15 happy solutions to the choreog-
16 raphy problem. Both Frederick
17 Ashton, who created "Patineurs"
18 from the music of Meyerbeer, and
19 David Lichine, who, along with
20 Johann Strauss, is responsible for
21 "Graduation Ball," have created

22 deft, animated ballets. Their stages
23 are consistently alive; their char-
24 acters are drawn vividly, and
25 with an urbane sort of wit, too
26 frequently absent from the me-
27 dium.
28   I have less difficulty containing
29 any enthusiasm for the "Nut-
30 cracker" excerpt and "Billy the
31 Kid," but this is not necessarily
32 the fault of the material. Wit-
33 nessing a pas de deux from a
34 full-length ballet is rather like
35 reading a chapter extracted from
36 the middle of a full-length novel;
37 things just don't quite jell. Al-
38 though the dancing of Nora Kaye
39 and Erik Bruhn was exquisite, I
40 could not avoid an impression of
41 incompleteness.
42   "Billy the Kid," ballet's answer
43 to the adult western, is, I sup-
44 pose, a harmless enough com-
45 modity. In fact, its very harm-

46 lessness rather undermines its ef-
47 fectiveness, for while Eugene
48 Loring's choreography showed
49 ample imagination—particularly
50 striking were the uses of lightings
51 and shadows—Aaron Copland's
52 score seemed so meek, tepid and
53 emotionally constricted that I
54 had to force my interest.
55–57 (*Here are named those "prom-*
inent in the various casts," with
praise.)
58   Once again, Kenneth Schermer-
59 horn and Sam Krachmalnick al-
60 ternated in the pit, and they
61 proved without a doubt that
62 young American conductors are
63 no less capable than their cousins
64 across the seas.
65   The ballet's final performance
66 here will be at 8:30 o'clock to-
67 night.
      —St. Louis (Mo.) *Post-Dispatch*

Analysis of the Review

The opening paragraph is typical of newspaper criticism of any art form: it immediately gives the reader the information about the who, what, when, where, and how, the why being obvious.

The critic then selects one number as a focus for his praise, setting the tone of the whole review. This is continued in the next two paragraphs, but somewhat less enthusiastically, and with certain reservations, as in lines 28 to 41 and 44 to 54.

Mr. Sasonkin concludes by naming the cast members he deemed to have given the best performances, singling out one for the greatest praise, sharing his compliments with the orchestra leaders, and ending on a dispensable paragraph about the final performance.

Note that in the opening paragraph he implies that "Les Patineurs" is a separate work from "Graduation Ball," but in the second paragraph says it is part of the latter, thus confusing his reader. The haste of news work is indicated in his resort to such stock expressions as "characters are drawn vividly," "urbane sort of wit," "things just don't quite jell," "striking use," and "proved without a doubt."

DRAMA

A performance by a local amateur group cannot be criticized exactly as one would review the same play if performed by a pro-

THE FOURTH ESTATE . . .   **By *Trent***

"Yes, but he's an excellent critic."

Courtesy, *Editor & Publisher*

fessional company in a Broadway theater. It is not that standards should be relaxed. But there should be appreciation of what the local group accomplishes with its resources. The professionals have many of the resources; the amateurs few. If the reviewer thinks home-town drama should be encouraged, he makes his adverse comments constructively—but he certainly makes them, for otherwise he is only a claque, an unpaid publicity man.

Critics working in big cities often must review plays without seeing the entire performance or on the basis of visiting a rehearsal. Planning the review helps greatly to overcome this handicap.

Play reviews, like those of other fiction, too easily produce involved plot summaries. A reader becomes bored with a passage like:

"Jane Acheson, the spinster heroine of this play, has problems with her young nieces and nephews. One day little Johnny Harper, the nephew from Bangor, Maine, comes to see her and decides he likes her town so much that he wants his parents to move to the village of Abercromie, setting for this play. So the Harper family, tyrannized by its son, moves to Abercromie. . . ." and so on.

A Review

By David Quinlan

1 In "The Remarkable Mr. Pen-
2 nypacker," a comedy which
3 opened last night at the Spa
4 Summer Theater, author Liam
5 O'Brien has presented for our
6 "conformist" era a 19th Century
7 picture of an individualist, as
8 logical as he is eccentric, at war
9 with sentiment and the world
10 of convention.

11 Mr. Pennypacker is equipped
12 with two families, one in Phila-
13 delphia and one in Wilmington,
14 Del., neither of which knows the
15 other exists until the time of the
16 play, which is set in Wilming-
17 ton in 1890.

18-26 (*A partial resume of the plot occurs here.*)

27 The funniest exchanges, per-
28 haps, are between the minister
29 and Pennypacker, in which Pen-
30 nypacker tries logically to relate
31 his action to Christian ethics.
32 The minister, a figure of impec-
33 cable respectability, attempts in
34 vain to defend his tenets.

35-46 (*This portion recounts two scenes from the play.*)

47 Burgess Meredith, as Pa Pen-
48 nypacker, realizes beautifully the
49 essential absurdity of his role—
50 that of a man at once immoral
51 and innocent, warmly affection-
52 ate and coldly reasonable, and,
53 above all, a man of hilarious ex-
54 pression.

55 John McGiver plays Dr. Fi-
56 field, the minister, as a pompous
57 but not unreasonable pillar of
58 convention, a vulnerable target
59 for Meredith.

60 Among other players, Wayne
61 Wilson, as Grampa Pennypack-
62 er, was easily the most profes-
63 sional, an acid and crotchety
64 soul. Iris Whitney played Ma
65 Pennypacker, properly bewil-
66 dered and indignant. The young-
67 er Pennypackers were mostly
68 unattractive and rather awkward
69 on stage, with the exception of
70 Barrie Delafiora, a youth of con-
71 siderable poise.

72 The set, designed by Sonia

73 Lowenstein, gave the proper air
74 of crusty Victorianism to the
75 proceedings. The picture of
76 Meredith working in these sur-
77 roundings is enough of a joke,
78 even if it weren't supported by
79 some of the funniest dialogue
80 around.
81–82 (*Notice of the next performance.*)
—Schenectady (N. Y.)
Union-Star

Analysis of the Review

The uses of narrative in critical writing are well shown in this review, which emphasizes plot. Mr. Quinlan assumes, wisely, that many of his readers are unfamiliar with the story. He recapitulates without revealing the solution.

Evaluation of the performances of those actors singled out for comment is impressionistic. Although a little reliant upon the worn verbiage of the news writer turned critic ("warmly affectionate and coldly reasonable," "pillar of convention," and "vulnerable target" are samples), the review shows insight and is discriminating in its opinions. Lines 72 to 80 offer highly original comment on an area often neglected by play critics.

A play of this type easily can move a critic to a political wisecrack that upsets the tone of the review. Mr. Quinlan avoided this temptation. Nor did he become so influenced by the evident absurdity of the play's situation that his review shows its jocularity with strain. The reviewer takes the play seriously, but not too seriously.

MOTION PICTURES

The movie, far more than the play and the dance, is a mass medium. Although attendance has fallen off in recent years, it still keeps more than 18,000 theaters in business. Three facts affect the writer in this area. They are: (1) the great American middle classes, particularly teen-agers, attend these theaters; (2) the movie is considered primarily a source of amusement; and (3) national distribution and frequent revivals of films increase the possibility that readers of a review have seen or expect to see the picture.

For some years books, mostly novels, have been a source of stories for movies. The movie critic, therefore, may incline to review the picture as he would the book, failing to see that the two are separate arts. Stage plays, of course, have since the beginning of the cinema industry been drawn upon for plots. Similarly, the movie critic may mistakenly review the movie version as he would write about the stage production. That writing about movies should differ is illustrated by Tom F. Driver, drama and movie reviewer for *The Christian Century,* in an extensive comparison of the stage and screen versions of *The Brothers Karamazov,* which he saw within 24 hours of each other. He wrote in part:

"What one misses in the stage version is all those details of time, place, and furnishing—details of consciousness—which serve the novelist in his task of probing the internal awareness of his characters. The play possesses the objective concerns of the novel without its subjective realization. The movie camera—by nature free, roving, and as greedy for detail as the mind of the novelist —succeeds better in realizing the subjective, psychological qualities of the book and its characters; but, for whatever reason, it fails to stick by the moral intent of its source. Perhaps the best result of both the play and the film will be that they renew interest in the novel itself, where the subjective and the objective are so magnificently integrated."

The mass appeal of the movie and television, also, subjects the reviewer to moral pressures, either within the publication office or from readers with decided views on what shall be put on the screen. Mrs. Marjorie Turner, onetime motion-picture editor and critic for the Syracuse *Herald-Journal,* faced this problem. She pointed out, in one of her articles in her paper, after being criticized by an anonymous letter writer because she did "not take a screaming stand against such pictures as 'The Moon Is Blue' and 'The French Line,' " that "In the pattern under which our society operates, adults are free to seek their own level in motion picture entertainment." She went on to observe that "The protection of children rests, after legal standards of decency are met, upon the home, the church, and those responsible for their training." She insisted that "It is fair to state on occasion that certain films are inappropriate for children, which does not mean they are immoral. A newspaper entertainment section is not a board of censorship."

If a critic desires a guide to standards and wishes to review movies from this point of view, he can obtain from the National Board of Review of Motion Pictures, Inc., New York, a concise summary that touches on Mrs. Turner's problem as well as others. It is titled, "Some Principles for Judging a Motion Picture."

A Review

(The review begins with the full indicia)

1 Hen's teeth are as rare as good
2 comedies nowadays so "Teacher's
3 Pet" at the Palace Theater has
4 something to preen its feathers
5 about. Hollywood used to be
6 quite proficient at this type of
7 movie, but the species is almost
8 extinct and you have to grab one
9 whenever it flashes by. If you feel
10 like a pleasant and relaxing two
11 hours, be sure and grab this one.
12 Clark Gable, of course, pio-
13 neered the genre with "It Hap-
14 pened One Night" some umpteen
15 years ago, and he has lost none
16 of his charm, suavity or timing.
17 While no Ted Giddings, he makes
18 the part of the city editor reek
19 with authentic journalistic know-
20 how. As the boys in the city room
21 used to say, he is tough but fair.
22 Doris Day has developed into
23 a full-fledged actress capable of
24 handling any part, and she pho-
25 tographs cuter than any female in
26 the world. Her flair for comedy
27 is delectable, and although she
28 must hew a fairly straight line
29 through most of the picture, she
30 makes the most of the few se-
31 quences where she is allowed

32 some leeway.
33-36 (*A partial summary of the plot follows.*)
37 and the script by Fay and
38 Michael Kanin is funny and in-
39 teresting without getting cute or
40 gimmicky. Producer William
41 Perlberg has created a solid New
42 York newspaper background, and
43 the technical credits are all first
44 rate. Director George Seaton has
45 concocted some beautiful touches,
46 and keeps things moving briskly
47 between editions.
48-50 (*Brief comments on others in the cast.*)
51 Producer Perlberg received
52 quite a bit of publicity when
53 making the picture by hiring
54 some 85 newspaper people
55 throughout the country to serve
56 as background personnel and
57 make everything look as authen-
58 tic as possible. He convinced me.
59 With one exception, the men are
60 ugly enough and the women suf-
61 ficiently homely to have come
62 from this very office.

—Milton R. Bass, in the
Pittsfield (Mass.)
Berkshire Eagle

Analysis of the Review

This review was selected because it deals with a movie about journalism as well as because it illustrates certain characteristics of newspaper film reviewing. Mr. Bass indulges in many of the colloquialisms reviewers often think they must use if they are to be in rapport with their readers ("grab one," "be sure and grab this one," "without getting cute or gimmicky," "photographs cuter than any female in the world").

Mr. Bass opens the review attractively with a switch on an old saying. He also uses the "you" style in the first paragraph but forgets about it subsequently: the mark of the slapdash writing of journalism.

The first two paragraphs are not so much about *Teacher's Pet* as about this type of film; the critic clearly uses the authoritarian approach. From there he goes on to comment upon the feminine lead and her part in the story, moving next into plot summary, combining brief résumé with opinion on its success.

Bright bits from the film then are described. The final paragraph is an irrelevant but revealing side light and gives the reviewer the opportunity for a quip. Hundreds of reviews of this film were written by newspaper people, and a number took this authoritative approach to it.

Music

Music critics' problems differ from those of the others, except critics of architecture, painting, and sculpture, because the art has more experimenters and innovationists than do the theater, movie, literature, photography, radio, television, and the dance. Dr. William Fleming, musician, music critic, and teacher at Syracuse University, once observed to a class of the author's students that "The new generation sees things that may not have been there originally. It reads into them, it re-interprets them in terms of today. Each age seems something different in each work of art. The critic can point out the trends."

The music critic must learn how to listen. His eyes help him little at a recital or concert. The complexity of the problem is indicated by the mechanical attempts to overcome it: Carter Harman, *Time*'s music editor, played tape recordings of concerts heard by the magazine's correspondents, using high fidelity and binaural machines so that he could become familiar with original works played outside New York. From the pages of the same magazine in 1956 comes a description of an electronic machine invented by a pianist, Jan Holcman, to enable him to judge "the technical abilities of a pianist." Despite these efforts, it is a common experience to read reviews of the same musical event, only to note that the critics seemed to have heard quite different music. The Chicago *Tribune* once analyzed the reviews of a Chicago Symphony Orchestra concert written by Olin Downes, James Whittaker, Miles Kastendienk, Oscar Thompson, Virgil Thomson, Samuel Chotzinoff, Pitts Sanborn, and Henry Simon and produced an amusing editorial about how differently the same sounds were heard by each.

A Review

By William Fleming

1 An ovation plus a chorus of
2 bravos hailed the final notes of
3 the Budapest String Quartet last
4 evening in Lincoln Auditorium
5 where it played under the spon-
6 sorship of the Famous Artists
7 Series.
8 Well-known through their re-
9 cordings, as well as from previ-
10 ous appearances here, the Buda-
11 pesters' mastery is complete.
12 Whether it was the brooding mu-
13 sic of Brahms, the Parisian gaie-
14 ties of Milhaud, or the ethereal
15 purity of Mozart, the ensemble
16 always sounded the right stylistic
17 note.
18 Suave and persuasive at all
19 times, the group seemed to play
20 with greater emotional warmth
21 and more intensity of concentra-
22 tion than on previous hearings.
23 Transparency of texture, econ-
24 omy of motion, and spic and span
25 cleanliness of line marked each
26 measure. Though the program
27 was largely unfamiliar, the dedi-
28 cation, devotion and skill with

29 which each phrase was fashioned
30 assured the rapt attention of a
31 large audience.
32 The string quartet, ever since
33 the 18th century, has been the
34 favored medium of so many of
35 the great masters for their most
36 intimate and philosophical pro-
37 nouncements. Small in volume
38 and slender in its silhouette, the
39 ensemble can be as large in its
40 expressive range as it is small in
41 size. Let the ear follow which-
42 ever of the four flowing strands
43 of sound it will, and there is al-
44 ways a wealth of music to be
45 found.
46–60 (*The reviewer comments, with
praise, systematically upon the
playing of each number.*)
61 As an encore, in response to the
62 enthusiastic applause, the group
63 played a movement from
64 Haydn's Quartet No. 46, thus
65 bringing the evening to a fitting
66 close with a tribute to the found-
67 ing father of the quartet medium.
—Syracuse (N. Y.)
Post-Standard

Analysis of the Review

Dr. Fleming combined the who-what-where information with a report on audience reaction. This device for starting a music or any other review sets a positive tone and also gratifies those

who were present by the reference to them. They, after all, are
the readers to count upon.

From there Dr. Fleming goes into high praise of the quartet's
playing of this specific concert, resorting to a few reviewer's
clichés now and then (lines 16 to 25, 30, 40, 61 to 62). He continues to remember the audience.

The fourth paragraph draws upon his knowledge as a musi-
cographer. Then, typical of the journalist, he begins all over
again, going back to the start of the program, dropping in a little
background here and there, a little criticism of the individual
artists, and a bit more history (lines 66 and 67).

Painting and Sculpture

The reviewer of these and other visual arts has a problem unlike those of his colleagues who deal with books, which, being
always in type, have a more or less fixed physical form. The critic
need not worry whether a book is set in Baskerville or Bodoni,
the jacket printed in pink or brown ink.

But the reviewer of an exhibit of paintings has to watch for
many different points on which he is expected to have something
to say: the quality of color, the pigments used, techniques employed in laying it on the canvas, the portrayal, if any, of reality,
the meaning (if intended), method of presentation, artistic philosophy, the context in which the work appears, the painting's
frame, its lighting, the jury decisions, and the type of work. In
an exhibit of from two to three hundred paintings (or works of
sculpture) the complexity of the task is obvious. This makes for
diffuseness in writing, for a preponderance of listings of names,
titles, and awards.

Writers for journalism on painting and sculpture often must
give considerable news emphasis to their reviews, since productions are shown in galleries, museums, and other exhibition places
open only between certain dates and hours. The public can more
easily hear original music and radio, see films, television shows,
drama, books, and the dance, having many opportunities for
direct contact with these arts. But sculpture, painting, and such
subdivisions as ceramics, are limited in display and therefore

not so accessible. Hence the reviewer tends to be more a reporter than he need be for the other arts.

Along with music, this has been the area of unrestrained criticism. Edna Woolman Chase and Ilka Chase, in *Always in Vogue*, their biography of Edna Chase, for many years editor of *Vogue* magazine, record a typical situation in the world of art criticism.

> The exhibition opened and the critics had a field day. They bared their fangs, sharpened their claws and sprang upon the prey. They looked out of Derain's "Window" and cried "Impossible." Cézanne's portrait of his wife was "Second Rate Impressionism." Of Redon's "Silence," the shadowy face with fingers on its lips, Kenyon Cox remarked that it certainly "makes insanity pay." *The Evening Post* stared at Van Gogh's self-portrait and pronounced it "Rubbish." Twenty-two years later, in 1935, a hundred and 26 thousand people would queue up in front of the Museum of Modern Art waiting their turn to view the great Van Gogh exhibition.

A Review

1 It is possible to be both elated
2 and highly disappointed in view-
3 ing the biennial Iowa Amateur
4 Art exhibit which officially opens
5 today in the public library art
6 gallery.
7 There is a small group of ex-
8 cellent paintings—strong, signifi-
9 cant and timeless; and there is a
10 very large group of paintings that
11 have nothing much to say.
12 This latter group abounds with
13 Iowa landscapes and barns, some
14 fairly well executed but few with
15 any impact or individualism.
16 Perhaps this is usually true of
17 a showing of amateur art—yet
18 the gap between the fine works
19 and the ones that just don't have
20 much guts has not seemed so
21 wide and so glaring in the past.
22 Is this indicative of a trend

23 in amateur art in Iowa? Is there
24 a tendency among amateur ar-
25 tists in this area to paint and re-
26 paint representative scenes that
27 have no force other than pictorial
28 pleasantry?
29 It may be an unfair generaliza-
30 tion to assume such a trend from
31 this one showing. Yet there have
32 been shades of such a trend noted
33 at the All-Iowa fair and the Iowa
34 State fair exhibits last summer.
35 Therefore, the above questions
36 need to be asked and pondered.
37 No blanket criticism of Iowa
38 landscapes and barns is intended
39 in the questions. Painting such
40 scenes and learning to master
41 them is an important aspect in
42 the schooling and development of
43 an artist. And it is from amateur
44 artists that we get our profes-

⁴⁵ sionals and those who will repre-
⁴⁶ sent the state in the near and dis-
⁴⁷ tant future.
⁴⁸   As in the past, this showing
⁴⁹ provides evidence of the tremen-
⁵⁰ dous wealth of art talent in Iowa.
⁵¹ We will not be at a loss for fine
⁵² artistic representation if that tal-
⁵³ ent grows and develops to some
⁵⁴ degree of its potential.
⁵⁵   What it seems to need more
⁵⁶ than anything else is the force
⁵⁷ of individualism, the force of rep-
⁵⁸ resenting the impressions, the
⁵⁹ emotions and the analyses of the
⁶⁰ artist himself on his subjects.
⁶¹   The small group of good paint-
⁶² ings in the show do this. And
⁶³ there is gratification in the char-
⁶⁴ acter and strength of some of the
⁶⁵ portraits.
⁶⁶   But the gap mentioned above

⁶⁷ should be of concern for Iowa
⁶⁸ artists. It should present an in-
⁶⁹ spiring and invigorating challenge
⁷⁰ —a challenge to paint with back-
⁷¹ bone as well as with hands,
⁷² brushes, and knives.
⁷³   One of the greatest values of
⁷⁴ exhibits such as this one, spon-
⁷⁵ sored by the Cedar Rapids Art
⁷⁶ Association, is that it offers an
⁷⁷ opportunity to note and evaluate
⁷⁸ the direction our young and aspir-
⁷⁹ ing artists are taking. If there is
⁸⁰ some question about that direc-
⁸¹ tion it can be brought to light
⁸² and discussed.
⁸³   *Awards for the show will be*
⁸⁴ *announced at a tea at 3 P.M.,*
⁸⁵ *Sunday, March 26.*
        —Donald D. Key, in the
        Cedar Rapids (Iowa) *Gazette*

Analysis of the Review

Even a quick reading shows that Mr. Key has gone far beyond the conventional review in this evaluation. His report is an editorial rather than a standard review of the sort that gives details about the paintings and news of the show.

Being primarily opinion makes it exceptional, whether or not we agree with his analysis. Few home-town newspaper reviews of local art shows would dare to be so adversely critical. Yet the criticism is constructive (lines 31 to 47 and 66 to 82). It avoids picking out any particular artists but gives a clue to them (lines 13, 14, 24 to 28, 37 to 43). Nor does it condemn regional art as such.

The news aspects are kept to a minimum (lines 1 to 6 and 83 to 85), and the last sentence was set in italics to separate it from the review, making the latter even more of an essay. Note the extreme shortness of paragraphs and the simplicity of language; in a few spots (lines 19, 68 to 72) it is hardly artistic and fitting, perhaps.

PHOTOGRAPHY

Except in a few books and specialized magazines, little critical writing on this art appears in print. Among the few publications for the general public that attempt to evaluate photography is the New York *Times*. Such magazines as *Popular Photography* and *Modern Photography* are the best sources for intensive criticism.

The problems of the photography critic are much like those of the painting critic, for he too is expected to comment on many different works. Since this is a nation of camera clickers, he has a large potential readership, but the practice of reviewing photography is undeveloped in popular American journalism and his is a small audience. The most competent criticism, some of which is first written for oral presentation, occurs in the meetings of camera clubs when judges give and explain their decisions on contest winners.

A Review

By Jacob Deschin

Photography of the underprivileged child can be a revelation of childhood in distress, or it can merely approach the maudlin for a propaganda effect. One is the reporter's way to communicate with simple directness the fact and emotion of a real situation; the other is almost always recognized for what it is—an obviously calculated effort to evoke a sympathetic response, and therefore, nearly always lacks conviction.

"Chim's Children," an exhibition at Limelight Gallery, 91 Seventh Avenue South, by the late David Seymour, who was Chim to his friends, is in effect a touching memorial to the photographer's love of children and concern for their welfare. That these pictures are also a photojournalist's report of what he found on his various assignments, during the Spanish Civil War, at Port Said, throughout Europe, is only incidental.

The pictures are personal, part of a large international picture album of his favorite subject, reflecting a lifelong devotion based on understanding and affection. The predominant mood is one of desperation, but there is enough in lighter mood to somewhat balance things off and to suggest an atmosphere of hopefulness.

Aside from a brief statement at the start of the display there are no captions and no identification as to place or event. Such information would have been superfluous at this show. For the pictures make a universal statement, as applicable in one circumstance as in another, anywhere in the world: Children in trouble and how they react to their plight.

⁵⁰ With the late Robert Capa ⁵¹ and the French photographer ⁵² Henri Cartier-Bresson, Mr. Sey- ⁵³ mour was one of the founders of ⁵⁴ Magnum, the international pho- ⁵⁵ tojournalists' cooperative, and ⁵⁶ president of the organization ⁵⁷ when he died. He was killed by ⁵⁸ Egyptian troops when his jeep ⁵⁹ crossed the cease-fire line be- ⁶⁰ tween Anglo-French and Egyp- ⁶¹ tian forces.

—New York *Times*

Analysis of the Review

Mr. Deschin undertakes the dangerous procedure of beginning with a philosophical generalization, relating his observation to journalism. His first paragraph, however, is necessary background for his review of a whole gallery of pictures.

The journalistic facts about the photo show are brought in later than is usual in newspapers.

The third paragraph shows a familiarity with the photographer's career and ties in with the lead. This material is followed by what appears to be adverse criticism but turns out to be praise, and once again relates to the exhibit's theme as well as to that of the review.

The critic concludes with biographical facts about the photographer, material that could be spared because it overbalances the piece with journalism. The review contains little evaluation, but enough (lines 30 to 37, 44) to keep it from being purely reportorial. It was accompanied by a two-column reproduction of one of the pictures.

RECORDINGS

Jacques Barzun is credited with having said: "A man is an ass who thinks of going into a shop and using his own ears, long or short, in selecting a disc." This remark is subject to many interpretations; certainly it points to the need for guidance for listeners in a time when millions of recordings are available and when even their types have become complex, as a result of the various speeds and numerous devices on which to play them.

Another problem for the recordings reviewer is that while almost all records are of music, and if he knows music he is equipped with an important portion of the knowledge he must possess (the remainder being knowledge of how recordings are made and marketed), the time is coming when he must be versatile enough to give sound judgments on readings of poetry and prose, choral speech, and other less common materials for discs.

He is more beset than most of his critical colleagues by the advertising and promotion departments of his publication, for the many record outlets in a community can be induced to advertise. Or he may be willing, without adequate technical knowledge, to review records "mainly just to get the records," as one reviewer honestly put it to the author. (One suspects that this motivates many a book reviewer as well.)

A further problem is that record producers are generous with review copies and the output is vast. Unlike book reviewers, recordings reviewers seem to feel impelled to comment on everything received; as a result, numerous publications run many inches of tightly packed, superficial comments.

A Review

1   All the late quartets, including the "Grosse Fuge,"
2 in one album. Proper digestion for review should take
3 months—or years, ideally. It is almost sacrilegious
4 to generalize a few words about such a limitless body
5 of musical expression.

6   As compared with other groups notable for these
7 works, especially the Budapest over many years,
8 the Hollywood achieves a commendable beauty of
9 tone and smoothness of ensemble. The pitch is un-
10 usually accurate in many spots that often are merely
11 approximated by other hard-pressed fiddlers. The in-
12 terpretations here are highly intelligent, well-thought-
13 out, accurate.

14   But, perhaps because of this, the playings are clearly
15 low-key—speaking relatively—sweeter but milder
16 than others we have heard. Not really mild—the
17 music allows no such thing. Just less craggy, the de-
18 tails of phrasing and feeling less energy-packed than
19 in the Budapest style of presentation.

20   Beautiful quartet string sound in the recording,
21 immersed in a big liveness.

        —Edward Tatnall Canby, in *Harper's* magazine

Analysis of the Review

The indicia indicate that this review covers the late quartets of Beethoven and offer the basic facts about the pressing.

Mr. Canby opens and closes with incomplete sentences, a common practice in a series of short reviews of any art. The quoted criticism was one of several under one heading.

His second paragraph is distinctly authoritarian, for he compares the work of the Hollywood String Quartet, which cut this disc, with that of the Budapest. So also are lines 17 to 19.

For so short a review there is about as much reference to the quality of the recording as can be expected; this is crammed into the final paragraph. In general this reviewer writes much like a music critic.

RADIO AND TELEVISION

Versatility has been demanded of the critics of all the arts so far considered, but it is by far of greatest importance for the radio and television reviewer. He must be capable of criticizing everything—acting, direction, photography, staging, casting, writing, music, news, sports, or any other subject matter visible or invisible on the set. This accounts in part for the inadequacies charged against criticism of this medium, such as that from within television itself voiced by Eric Sevareid, who wrote in *The Reporter:*

". . . television could do with a sharp drop in the quantity of criticism and a sharp rise in its quality. How many writers who haven't read a play since Booth Tarkington's 'Seventeen' are posing as critics of TV drama? . . . How many boy graduates who can't tell a test tube from a peavey hook are instructing TV networks in the right and wrong of their science programs?"

Another problem is that only the people who have seen a television performance pay much attention to criticisms after the event. But the public does follow the advance reviews available in newspapers. (See Chapter 10.)

The repeat possibilities of a TV show are not so great as, say, with books, which remain in circulation indefinitely and make recording of opinion on them sufficiently important to support such a publication as the *Book Review Digest*. Numerous critics, aware of this dilemma, do not write reviews for publication the day after a show. "I prefer," the author learned from Donald Freeman, radio-television critic and editor of the San Diego *Union* and the Copley News Service syndicate, "to do the essay type of review which doesn't get stale, theoretically, and can run in other papers a few days later."

There are other problems more or less peculiar to these media —contending with a deluge of publicity material, writing for a heterogeneous audience, dealing with more mail than critics of the other arts generally receive, and, because these media are relatively new, having few resources to provide background.

If *hoi polloi* describes the readers of any part of the critical content of the popular press, it is the radio-television portion. Knowing this, the critic keys down his style, assumes an informality, even slanginess, of tone that would not do for the book, music, or art critic (outside of *Variety* and *The Billboard*).

Robert Sokolsky, entertainment editor of the Syracuse *Herald-Journal*, pointed out, in a talk to one of the author's critical writing classes, that the critic aware of this mass audience faces certain other pitfalls. One is overwriting, dwelling at too great length on a subject; another is egotism, which may result in writing down to people; another is pontificating; still another is "showing one's intelligence instead of serving the public"; yet one more is "not taking responsibility seriously." On this last he pointed out that the public responds vigorously to what the critic writes and that the critic might well ask himself each day: "Is it worth it to say what I'm going to say?"

A Review

By Donald Freeman

1 Sal Mineo, everyone's favorite
2 tire-stripper and switch-blade
3 wielder, turned up the other night
4 in the role of Aladdin, a bit of
5 casting with a formidable shock
6 value. In his relatively brief
7 career, Mineo—let's face it—has
8 played enough juvenile delin-
9 quents to fill an honor farm. Sal
10 Mineo in the "Arabian Nights"?
11 It did take quite a while for the
12 shock to dissipate itself.
13 Once this hurdle was done
14 with, however, one could settle
15 down and enjoy this dazzling,

16 90-minute television version of
17 the story about a boy and his
18 magic lamp.
19   It wasn't exactly the fairy tale
20 that you and I know, not this
21 eye-popper. "Aladdin," as pic-
22 tured on the CBS "Show of the
23 Month" series, proved to be an
24 extravagantly mounted musical
25 comedy with music by that old
26 city slicker, Cole Porter, and a
27 script by S. J. Perelman, who
28 hasn't been behind a plow in
29 some time himself.
30   In short, this particular "Alad-
31 din" was markedly on the sleek,
32 sophisticated side. Actually, to
33 borrow a fact from CBS pub-
34 licity, the "Aladdin" story is
35 about 800 years old and there
36 are at least a dozen variations
37 afloat. For this tale Mr. Perel-
38 man merely took the most dra-
39 matic elements in each of the
40 different versions.
41   What Mr. Perelman ended up
42 with was a yarn as improbable

43 as all fairy stories but with a
44 good deal more wit and verve
45 than most.
46   Wildly comic, stilted, satiric
47 and richly embroidered, the Per-
48 elman prose felt right at home
49 in the royal court of ancient
50 Pekin. . . .
51–61 (*Here occurs an illustration from the dialogue.*)
62   As for the musical score, it
63 was Mr. Porter's very first for
64 TV. The birth of any new Porter
65 score is a significant event, of
66 course. But on first hearing,
67 which is hardly conclusive, I'm
68 forced to say this one did seem
69 a cut below his standard. Still,
70 even a near-miss from Cole Por-
71 ter rates far ahead of the field
72 and both his tunes and his lyrics
73 were entirely serviceable.
74–88 (*The critic comments on the audience aim and then concludes with short comments on the remainder of the cast.*)
—San Diego (Calif.) *Union*

Analysis of the Review

Before he joined the *Union,* the critic was a sports writer for the Chicago *Tribune.* The sports reporter's common practice of using synonyms is demonstrated in the opening paragraph, especially lines 1 and 2. In sports language a ball is a ball only once in the same article, thereafter a sphere, spheroid, globe, pellet, or "the leather," to use only a few of the dozens of substitutes. This adds variety and brightness to all of Mr. Freeman's copy, for he does not overdo the practice.

Like all who write about radio and television, this critic did not need much space in which to present the journalistic essentials, which are fed in gradually even to the middle of the review.

Criticism in earnest begins at the third paragraph and is maintained at about the same rate to the end. The center portion is devoted to what only the more sophisticated readers and viewers would appreciate: the contribution of Perelman, the humorist, who, while popular, is not known to the man-on-the-street TV viewer. In this section Mr. Freeman makes evident his awareness that, while the show might be mistaken for one intended to be seen by children, it was developed with so much sophistication that the humor angle deserved comment. It is dealt with humorously in lines 19 to 29.

Writing the Critical Article

Writing a critical article is a major test of a critic's abilities. The book review, the drama criticism, or the evaluation of some other single production, at least in these times, is a relatively short piece of writing. Often as not it is no more than a few hundred words.

But the article not only is more extensive than the review; it also is more intensive, more penetrating and analytical. In it the writer cannot stop with mainly describing or reporting; he also must dissect. Early in this century, when a book review frequently was also a critical article (the book being only an excuse for a long dissertation), this distinction was not so clear. But today the difference is sharp. Few reviewers are given either the time or the space in which to dilate upon their subjects.

Idea- Versus Thing-Mindedness

The writer of the critical article for the mass media must be dominantly idea-minded, as opposed to thing-minded. This distinction, made for general journalistic purposes, was made years ago by two writers and journalism teachers, Harry F. Harrington and Lawrence Martin. They used to point it out to their students at Northwestern University.

Some persons, they explained, react most strongly to things; "i.e., to persons, facts, events." Others, however, "attend more spontaneously to ideas, notions, generalizations, thoughts about things." They decided that most story writers and poets are thing-minded; most philosophers, essayists, and critics are idea-minded. Harrington and Martin asked their students to answer these questions about themselves:

"The test is, are you interested in ideas, in interpretations, in abstract relations, as such? When you discover an apparently new idea, are you thrilled? Would you rather write narrative or exposition? What sort of books do you read for pure pleasure: travel and fiction, or essays and critical and controversial works?"[1]

They go on to say that a thing-minded person is not so likely to do well in an editorial position as an idea-minded one. He can hold a job but will not be able to excel as readily as the other. They admit, too, that some persons are equally thing- and idea-minded, suggesting Bernard Shaw, H. G. Wells, and G. K. Chesterton as noted examples.

We might put it this way: the reporter gives pictures of persons, things, and events in writing. The critic explains, relates, and analyzes them and points to opinions and conclusions resulting from this cerebration.

The writer of the critical article, therefore, should be idea-minded. For here the full play of his response is to be read. This response is not a quickie, such as he must give when covering a single performance, especially if he has not seen it in rehearsal. The superficiality of his reaction is most extreme when a critic cannot even stay through a play, say, which he did not see rehearsed and must leave at the end of the second act. The critical article is a careful composition that evaluates and appreciates the whole body of a writer's work, the whole career of a singer, or the complete field, such as an article that might be written under the title, "The Development of a Tradition of American Ballet."

The Article Defined

The article, like the essay, is difficult to define, for it has no special form, as does a news story. It resembles the essay in that it, too, is a short piece of prose, with less emphasis on style, and

[1] Harrington, Harry F., and Martin, Lawrence: *Pathways to Print*. New York, Van Nostrand, 1931, p. 168.

wider purpose. It may be intended to inform, guide, entertain, or/and influence. Actually it is a collection of facts or ideas assembled to gratify one or more of these intentions. If it is to appear in a magazine, where it usually does, it must fit the needs of the magazine concerned.

Almost none of the analysts of the modern article for either the newspaper or the magazine gives place to the classification *critical article*. Harrington and Martin devote a few lines to it. The only longer treatment is that of Brennecke and Clark in their book, and that is more extensive only in that others say so little. They confine themselves to the critical article dealing with books, and their example is a sort of omnibus review-criticism covering five autobiographies at once.

The critical article is likened by them to a discussion article concerning politics or some other debated subject. And what is a discussion article? They say: "When interest is about equally divided between the facts and inferences, the result is what we call a 'discussion article.'" Bird, in his *Article Writing and Marketing*, appears to include the discussion article in his classification called argumentatives and essays. A finer distinction is necessary. Many a discussion (also critical) article does not argue; it simply exposes or explains.

A critical article, then, is a piece of prose which ranges from several thousand to eight or ten thousand words in length, is intended to analyze some phase of the arts, and attempts to evaluate them.

Writing the Article

Whatever it may be called or however it may be classified, the important information for a writer is how to produce the critical article. In fundamental method it is no different from any other. The following steps are followed by students and professionals alike.

1. The writer is endowed with an idea or is given an idea by an editor; i.e., he obtains a topic or subject for the article.

2. He gathers facts and opinions relating to that subject.

3. He analyzes and relates these facts and produces new ideas pertaining to the general purposes of the article. If he is an average writer in his methods, he uses cards or notebooks in which to place these materials; the exceptional journalist does much of this sorting and relating in his head as he looks over his notes, clippings, letters, and other sources.

4. He prepares an outline. A slow but dependable method is to list words, phrases, and sentences that represent all the different items that will go into the article, regardless of relationship or order. This list is then analyzed in turn, the related items being grouped. The author of this book uses 3″ x 5″ white cards in note-taking; these are then easy to spread out on a large table or on the floor and arrange in any desired order. If the article writer's purpose is clearly in mind, the outline will begin to take shape as he fits each bit of information to that purpose. It often is desirable to write a paragraph setting forth the purpose of the article, as a starter.

5. He designs an attractive opening or ending. Sometimes the precise content of these two important segments of the article has been determined long before outlining. A strong news-peg (news event relating to the general subject of the article) will win out over many another opening, as for example the critical evaluations of George Jean Nathan when he died in 1958. The third paragraph of *Newsweek*'s article on him read: "When Nathan died last week at 76, full of honors, he was hailed as the unquestioned dean of American drama critics. But he was more than that." The timely reference for John Mason Brown's article on Nathan was provided when the New York *Times* subtitled his article with "The Late George Jean Nathan: Wizard of Verbal Cactus." The main title was "Critic's View of a Critic."

The ending often grows naturally from the beginning or from the main theme of the article. The ending may repeat the beginning, to clinch the idea, or be an anecdote which emphasizes the chief message of the article.

6. The writer next develops methods of presenting his materials for the body of the article. Whichever method is used may,

in fact, affect the fifth step, the selection of beginning and ending. A writer may use the deductive (general to the particular) or the inductive (particular to the general) architecture for the article.

Under the deductive the writer starts with minor details, goes to major ones, returns to minor details, and then recapitulates the opening. If he uses the inductive method the sequence offers a choice of two arrangements. One is to start with a general statement that follows an example or incident, then provide minor and major details, all leading to a general restatement of the original proposition. The second is to begin with minor details and work up to the general proposition, which is not stated anywhere except at the end, as a sort of conclusion. At the end of this chapter is an article which shows the latter method of plan for a critical article; it is entitled "The Journalist as Autobiographer."

7. After an indefinite number of drafts, the article finally is retyped, read aloud to someone, retyped as necessary, and submitted, along with whatever pictures or art work have meantime been obtained. A query, that is, a letter to an editor, proposing the article and seeking to arouse his interest in it, often is desirable before starting to write, but, since critical writing in the article field is concerned more with trends than with spot news, it is less necessary to prepare by the query method.

Typical Articles

If we examine the many critical articles that are all around us in magazines and newspapers, we find that some run as regular parts of publications. Others, however, appear under headlines and titles as special features or special articles. For many years work by J. Donald Adams has appeared every week on the second page of the New York *Times Book Review*. Usually this is a critical article, one of the shorter ones to be found regularly. Occasionally it is an essay or an editorial instead of an article. The editorial differs from the critical article in that it comes close to being propaganda, often is marred by bias, and fails to consider all sides of the subject. The competent article also takes a stand, but not until after presenting all sides of the subject: this is the virtue of the great length to which the critical article is allowed to run.

As this book was being prepared, typical article titles appeared in the publications which critics of the arts might often read. In *Harper's* Martin Mayer wrote on "The Budapest Quartet"; in *The New Republic* appeared "Paul Valery's da Vinci," by Malcolm Cowley; *Dissent* printed "Pop Culture and Kitsch Criticism," by Harold Rosenberg; *Partisan Review* presented Mary McCarthy's "Greene and God on Broadway." Anthony West used one book as the springboard for a critical article in *The New Yorker* and titled it vaguely enough as "Dusty Answer." *The Chicago Review* carried an article on "Nelson Algren and His Critics" by Lawrence Lipton. There were dozens more in *The Nation, The Atlantic, The Commonweal, The Christian Century, The Virginia Quarterly Review, Yale Review, The Saturday Review* and most of the "little" literary magazines (see Chapter 12).

John Lardner contributed "Notes on the Top Clown" in "The Air" department of *The New Yorker*. In this article he evaluated Sid Caesar's then new television show and used the method of comparing him with certain earlier comedians—Bobby Clark, W. C. Fields, and Jimmy Durante.

Carefully studying such articles helps the beginning writer immensely. His aim in the analysis is not to become a shadow of some other writer but to develop his own techniques after learning those of others who are successful. Picasso and Dali, for instance, were not always highly original; in their early years they learned to become excellent draftsmen and produce conventional work.

From analysis the writer learns that the design of a critical article (or any other) resembles that of the human being: it has a head, a body, and feet, more commonly called a beginning, a middle, and an end. To retain these distinctions these parts must be different: the head smaller than the body, the feet of different construction than either of the other two. And thus it is with the critical article. If it is planned to begin inductively, there are various choices for the opening. It may be an anecdote, an incident, a news-peg, an example which sets forth the detail, or a slight descriptive passage. For instance, Ernest J. Simmons began an article in *The Nation* about the writings of Boris Pasternack this way:

> When I met Boris Pasternack in the Soviet Union years ago, he was slender, of middle height, and his face, with its high cheekbones and staring eyes, bore a pained, neurasthenic expression. He was even then regarded by a few critics of discrimination as the greatest poet to emerge from the Soviet Revolution.

Or take this beginning, observed in the *Harper's* article describing and evaluating the work of the Budapest String Quartet:

> A telephone rang in the studio control room, cutting through the chromatics of a late Mozart string quintet which was playing at a high volume through the loudspeaker. Sascha (Alexander) Schneider picked up the receiver and said . . .

The construction of the anatomy or body of the article stems naturally from the type of beginning, thus unlike humans. Why unlike them? Because they may have small heads and fat bodies, or attractive heads and unattractive bodies. The article that begins with a generalization proceeds to supply the support for that generalization in its center or body.

Professional article writers sometimes write the core or center of an article before composing the opening and closing paragraphs, or vice versa. This method is more often used with the extraordinarily long article than one of a few thousand words, whose entire compass can be kept in mind and seen whole.

The magazines for the highly educated, the reviews for the sophisticated, and the journals for artists are by no means the sole outlets for the critical article. Scores of newspapers of general circulation also publish them. These include far more than the nationally distributed New York *Times,* New York *Herald Tribune,* and the *Christian Science Monitor* of Boston. Critical articles appear also (not so profusely as in the national newspapers) in the larger dailies of Chicago, St. Louis, Milwaukee,

Philadelphia, Los Angeles, San Francisco, Denver, Washington, Boston, Omaha, and Atlanta, among others. They also are used by numerous dailies in smaller cities, especially those with colonies of artists or university and college populations, such as Columbia, Missouri; Urbana, Illinois; Bethlehem, Pennsylvania; and both coastal Portlands. In most states there are a few art-conscious general weekly or country papers that are hospitable to such writing, although not many out of the total of about 9,000 such papers.

Only the dailies among the newspapers are likely to pay for critical articles in anything more negotiable than free copies. The beginning critical writer is wise to be willing to give his articles to the weeklies while he is in his apprenticeship, for at least it is publication and an opportunity to get response and criticism of his criticism. But he should give them away only if they are of strictly local interest, and if he is convinced that they are technically satisfactory as pieces of writing. Half-baked critical articles can harm an art or a performer and are best left unpublished.

Sources of Articles

Which brings us to the sources of articles. Where do they come from? When they appear in newspapers they frequently are the work of staff writers, but some are purchased from free lancers. The publications that have demonstrated genuine interest in the arts are the ones the unattached writer should approach.

When critical articles appear in magazines they are likely as not to have come from outside the staff, from specialists in the particular art form. About the only ones that do not pay for such writing are the "little" magazines, which cannot pay for anything more than the printer's work and the postage bill, and often fail to do even that and go out of business. Usually the highly competent newspaper critic of any art is found also contributing to the magazines that deal with that art; the reverse is true as well. John Mason Brown, the drama critic, writes for both newspapers and magazines; Walter Kerr criticizes that art for the New York *Herald Tribune* but also appears in *Harper's,*

The Commonweal, and other magazines as well as in books and also on television programs (although on the latter not so clearly as a critic as an analyst). The critic with a newspaper job writes for both newspapers and magazines, whereas the critic with a magazine post is likely to write for them and also to appear in book form, since the pace on magazines is slower and the quality of work done for them is more nearly of the quality needed for books. It is more long-range work than is newspaper copy.

Newspapers not only buy art-world news from syndicates but also critical articles; these usually are part of the budget of material contracted for. Another source is the public relations or publicity department of some art enterprise. An editor desiring an article about a museum, for example, can get it free from the public relations agency or advertising agency which has contracted to promote the museum. Not often is such an article a genuinely critical one; it is more likely to be a straight feature or a descriptive piece.

Critical articles are so much a personal expression by the writer that it is common for the better-known critics to arrange for publication in advance of writing or to receive assignments. This practice may account for the repetition of names or for one critic having his fingers in four or five different media at one time. So many of the arts receive first expression in New York City that it is natural for editors to turn to writers who work there, and the better ones are soon active in different journalistic media. It is a matter of geographical convenience, coupled with demonstrated ability at critical writing, that explains the apparent concentration.

Genesis of Two Articles

Users of this book are interested, presumably, in how actual critical articles are prepared. It should be useful, therefore, to trace the genesis and production of such articles. Two that were created in entirely different ways are analyzed in the remainder of this chapter.

The critical article sometimes is confused, especially by newspaper writers, with the feature story. Descriptive writing about artists or an art form is not critical writing. A biographical sketch of Mozart, tracing the chief outlines of his career, is a feature or a biographical article, but not a critical one. Analysis is a requisite. This qualification should be remembered in studying the two articles to follow, for both use sufficient straight factual material to mislead the casual reader who may overlook the critical expressions. Criticism should be measured, not by its extent or volume, but by its penetration and depth.

The origin of an article called "The Journalist as Autobiographer" was in the reading of a succession of books by newsmen and magazinists relating their experiences and chronicling their lives. The author's knowledge of the history of journalism made him realize that here was a new phase in biographical literature. In the nineteenth century, journalists often remained anonymous. Few of them published more than dull reminiscences, made up largely of letters to and from relatives, friends, and professional acquaintances. Franklin stood out as an exception. But in the twentieth century, when biographical and autobiographical writing received the impact of such authors as André Maurois and Lytton Strachey, the journalists who told their life stories began producing introspective books. Along came the popular *Personal History* by Vincent Sheean, to be followed by Walter Duranty's *I Write as I Please*, and others by Stephen Bonsal and Eugene Lyons. The article writer, in the course of reviewing these and many other books for various professional journals, began to see a trend.

The article was prepared by going through all the books of reminiscence and autobiography by journalists from Franklin on, taking notes and picking out quotations on the amount and nature of the self-examination and introspection each contained. These were put on 3" x 5" cards, and arranged in chronological order. The article fell naturally into a chronological pattern.

Next came thinking about how the trend or the particular change in the nature of journalistic autobiography came about. On other cards the factors involved in the change were set down, one by one, and explained. There also was an attempt to account for the reasons why the early journalists did not produce the type of literary material seen in the present century. This background was followed by a conclusion based on an attempt to show the ultimate meaning of this type of writing.

From the collection of cards and other materials an outline for the article was devised, although a rough scheme already was in the author's mind while collecting notes: the aim and purpose of the article had been decided beforehand. But now it was necessary to decide the exact arrangement of the units.

The cards, additional notes, clippings, and other pertinent documents thought to be useful, such as the reviews of the older books from the author's file, were then arranged on a large table. A sequence was decided upon, then changed in favor of the chronological. This change was made easily simply by rearranging the order of the cards.

Once the cards and other notes were in at least temporarily satisfactory order, the article writer prepared a first draft, directly on the typewriter. This was allowed to cool off for a few days. Then it was read carefully and edited. Another day or so of cooling, and the draft was rewritten, with new changes incorporated. It underwent various other changes even in the typing: new examples, new ways of saying what he had written occurred to the writer. This latest draft also was edited closely, and finally rewritten with still other alterations, mostly in the manner of expression.

The typescript was sent off to a national magazine of ideas, which promptly rejected it with a letter. It went to another such periodical, which sent it back in two weeks with a rejection slip as well. Five other periodicals also did not want it, all writing personal letters, and some with good reason for rejection, such as the fact that one of them went out of business the same month. The eighth to which it had been sent accepted it with enthusiasm and published it.

Soon after publication, the author received from the one magazine that had sent him a rejection slip instead of a personal letter a new communication from the editor. This letter praised the article and said that the editor would like to see some other work by the writer. In his reply, the author reminded this editor that he had had a chance to publish the article he now was praising and had refused it. This experience proved to the author in question that editors, like all the rest of us, do not always operate scientifically. He also decided that before doing extensive work on similar critical articles he would query editors first.

Here is the article as finally published, followed with notes about its construction. It is quoted, by no means as a model, but because no one knows its origin as well as the author. For the sake of brevity, some parts are omitted and their nature indicated.

THE JOURNALIST AS AUTOBIOGRAPHER[2]

By Roland E. Wolseley

1 If Dana and Greeley, those convenient symbols
2 of mid-nineteenth-century journalism, were here to-
3 day to see the flow of personal histories by reporters,
4 correspondents, and editors, they would write whole
5 newspaper pages in editorializing on the decay of the
6 press. For in their day anonymity was the rule, usu-
7 ally even for themselves, although it is true that many
8 readers knew who was writing. What these famous
9 editors would think, also, about the unrestrained use
10 now of signed articles in magazines and newspapers
11 cannot even be imagined.
12 There must be reasons for this growth in per-
13 sonalizing the journalist beyond a simple change in
14 journalistic mores or a growing lust for royalties.
15 The personalizing has shifted in recent years to the
16 relatively lower ranks from the mountainous region
17 where dwelt the editorial bigwigs. Today there is not
18 one but there are dozens of Richard Harding Davises,
19 modified, it is true, by the necessities of total war.
20 Journalists as authors of introspective books are
21 new. The great editors of the nineteenth century
22 would complain about that particularly. Candace

[2] Wolseley, Roland E.: "The Journalist as Autobiographer." *The South Atlantic Quarterly,* January, 1943, pp. 38–44. Reproduced by permission.

²³ Stone, describing the New York *Sun* under Dana,
²⁴ observes in her book, *Dana and the Sun,* that the
²⁵ paper was called "the graveyard of reputations" be-
²⁶ cause of "the impersonal character of the *Sun*." In
²⁷ those days the identity of authors was unrevealed.
²⁸ "Day after day," Miss Stone writes, "a staff member
²⁹ might write brilliant editorial or news articles only to
³⁰ have his achievement referred to in two words: 'Dana
³¹ says.' "
³²   Until Vincent Sheean published his *Personal His-*
³³ *tory* journalists rarely exploited themselves in their
³⁴ books. The first American newspaper writer of im-
³⁵ portance to discuss himself was Benjamin Franklin,
³⁶ whose *Autobiography* goes back to 1787, if French
³⁷ editions are accepted as the first. He set no vogue,
³⁸ for the next such publication of any significance was
³⁹ Joseph T. Buckingham's *Personal Recollections and*
⁴⁰ *Memoirs of Editorial Life.* Published in 1852, it
⁴¹ is almost unreadable without a magnifying glass and
⁴² a great curiosity about the many dry quotations on
⁴³ the activities of a now forgotten Boston editor. Buck-
⁴⁴ ingham's real name was Joseph Tinker. A vibrant
⁴⁵ Whig, he edited the Boston *Courier.* He was more
⁴⁶ literary than most of his fellow editors of the second
⁴⁷ quarter of the last century, once succeeding in per-
⁴⁸ suading Nathaniel Hawthorne to contribute to a
⁴⁹ literary magazine of which he was editor.
⁵⁰⁻¹⁰⁹ *(Lines 50 to 109 cover, in similar manner, the*
     work of Greeley, Brockway, Elizabeth Banks, and
     others.)
¹¹⁰   Two or three books were issued thereafter and
¹¹¹ even during the significant year 1934, when Sheean's
¹¹² *Personal History* was published. His book, although
¹¹³ not new in intent, was new in method, a method
¹¹⁴ which Steffens used slightly in his volumes. Until this
¹¹⁵ time when journalists wrote about themselves they
¹¹⁶ waxed largely historical or anecdotal. Edward P.
¹¹⁷ Mitchell, for years an austere editor of the New York
¹¹⁸ *Sun,* for example, told in his *Memoirs of an Editor*

119 familiar stories about that paper, offering pen por-
120 traits of his fellow editors in the somewhat weighty
121 manner of a Union League club member telling his
122 experiences at the Fiftieth Anniversary Banquet.
123 Julius Chambers described *News Hunting on Three*
124 *Continents* and threw in ghost stories for lagniappe.
125 No one worked very hard to correlate his material
126 or explain what all this activity might mean.

127   Sheean, however, added an ingredient which can
128 best be described as philosophical overtones. Begin-
129 ning with his analysis of college work in the opening
130 chapter, he realized the need for interpretation of
131 experiences as well as for recounting them. He was as
132 much concerned with explaining how he thought a
133 revolution had been born in Russia as with describ-
134 ing the action of the revolt itself. What his book did,
135 in addition, was to show the public that a journalist
136 did not have to rely on the often hasty writing of
137 his daily routine for the production of a book. Most
138 of the autobiographies by earlier journalists seemed
139 as if they had been written between covering stories
140 and snatching a snack, which probably is when they
141 were composed.

142   It took two years before this sank into the minds
143 of his fellow journalists, although the following year
144 Walter Duranty's *I Write as I Please* appeared. This
145 book has much in common with Sheean's in method,
146 but it is coincidence rather than influence that ex-
147 plains it, for both correspondents were introspective
148 journalists. When the technique made itself clear, the
149 flood of journalistic books began. Six were issued in
150 1936, one of them the late Webb Miller's widely read
151 *I Found No Peace.* Fourteen came out in 1937, in-
152 cluding volumes by Stephen Bonsal, Lilian Mowrer,
153 and Eugene Lyons. Eleven more followed the next
154 year, with women writers almost keeping pace with
155 the men. Pierre van Paassen and Oswald Garrison
156 Villard were among eleven more in 1939. In 1940
157 a new angle was taken; the country journalist began

158 to have his say. Again eleven was the number. Two
159 of the books were *Country Editor* and *Ink on My*
160 *Hands,* both by small-town editors.
161–181 (*Lines 161 to 181 discuss the work of Mencken,*
      Cobb, and other more recent journalists.)
182   We now come to the necessity to account for this
183 trend. There are more incisive explanations than say-
184 ing what is entirely true: that the success of books
185 like Sheean's and Duranty's and van Paassen's is
186 very tempting to any correspondent who has spent
187 a few hours watching the bombs fall on a European
188 city or Asiatic harbor.
189   The change in journalistic customs also is a factor,
190 of course. These days journalists see their by-lines
191 as commonplace; even writers of routine accident
192 stories find their initials on their news accounts in
193 New York *PM*. So common is the signed story that
194 nothing short of a regular personal column seems
195 to satisfy the newspaperman any more. H. Allen
196 Smith wrote features for the New York *World-Tele-*
197 *gram,* published a jaunty book (*Low Man on a*
198 *Totem Pole*), and was promoted to syndicated col-
199 umnist. Recently he was graduated from that into a
200 radio spot. Henry McLemore wrote humorous sport
201 stories for the United Press and made such a hit that
202 he, too, was signed by a syndicate to fill regular space
203 daily. In time, no doubt, he will rival another sports
204 writer who is a self-styled labor, political, and what-
205 not expert, Westbrook Pegler
206   That is the sort of career the journalist aspires to
207 these days, not the seat of Arthur Brisbane, with a
208 quarter of a million dollar salary and the responsibility
209 for writing simplifications of pseudo science for the
210 masses. Nor does he care to imitate Adolph Ochs,
211 who strove to cover the news of medicine as well as
212 of sport.
213   Another factor of a major nature is the point that
214 the journalist has become a person of parts in society,
215 or at least is on his way. Although it still lingers in

²¹⁶ England, despite the war and its leveling influence,
²¹⁷ the sneer at the reporter is passing from the faces of
²¹⁸ those who gaze upon him. At his best he can, like
²¹⁹ Leland Stowe, write books that sell in the thousands
²²⁰ of copies and deliver lectures for which he receives
²²¹ anywhere from $250 to $750 apiece. This is quite
²²² a contrast to the holding of the nose about journalism
²²³ as a career a century ago, when, as Miss Stone puts
²²⁴ it, "In those days, brilliant young men of good family
²²⁵ were not expected to choose newspaper careers. Jour-
²²⁶ nalism dictated irregular hours and association with
²²⁷ people of all types, and provided but a small remu-
²²⁸ neration."
²²⁹ Today journalists are likely to be graduates of gen-
²³⁰ eral colleges if not always of schools of journalism.
²³¹ Often they belong to a newspaper union, which has
²³² given them class consciousness. They have re-
²³³ sponded, also, to the sometimes undeserved label of
²³⁴ modern historian. The success of interpretative stud-
²³⁵ ies of current affairs by Gunther, Sheean, Negley
²³⁶ Farson, Edmond Taylor, William Shirer, and scores
²³⁷ of others has placed a glow around the more mun-
²³⁸ dane newspaperman who covers the city hall beat
²³⁹ and around the hard-working editorial assistant of
²⁴⁰ a magazine that publishes articles by these journal-
²⁴¹ istic big-shots. For better or worse, journalism is
²⁴² becoming more and more a profession and less and
²⁴³ less a racket or sport among vocations.
²⁴⁴ But this is not all. Careful reading of the old auto-
²⁴⁵ biographies and of such thorough historical treatises
²⁴⁶ on journalism in this country as Frank Luther Mott's
²⁴⁷ *American Journalism* and his three-volume study of
²⁴⁸ magazines will show the truth to be that few of the
²⁴⁹ old-timers were capable of writing the type of book
²⁵⁰ which today is common. The art of autobiographical
²⁵¹ and biographical writing simply had not developed
²⁵² far enough. Back in the eighties the concept of an
²⁵³ autobiography usually was a collection of letters with
²⁵⁴ sprinklings of simple biographical facts and random
²⁵⁵ impressions to unite them, all set in very small type

256 and running across two or three thick volumes, the
257 result put up in a dull and stodgy binding. They were
258 weary recollections indeed.

259   The interest of an autobiography depends very
260 much upon how well the author can reflect the life
261 he has led in words so well chosen as to obtain the
262 broadest comprehension of himself and his views. A
263 doctor who has had a remarkable career of public
264 service can write about himself in such a way as to
265 miss all the best possibilities; another doctor who
266 has lived a much less colorful life can prepare a book
267 which squeezes the most in the way of philosophical
268 observations, human interest, and drama out of his
269 career.

270   Whether pre- or post-Sheean, journalists who
271 write their autobiographies have the opportunity to
272 make the realities of journalistic life more clear, to
273 entertain with stories, and to inform thier readers
274 about widely- or little-known incidents in history.
275 The later or younger group has succeeded more often
276 in carrying out all these possibilities than in ignoring
277 them, which is more than can be said for autobiogra-
278 phers among businessmen and other citizens who live
279 more or less sedentary lives.

280   Although most of the recent autobiographies have
281 something to say, some admittedly are wishy-washy
282 and superficial. All the volumes divide into the act-
283 ing, the thinking, and the combination acting-think-
284 ing groups, whereas the older books usually were
285 acting only. A typical recent action autobiography
286 would be Linton Wells's *Blood on the Moon*. An
287 example of the more thoughtful type is William Henry
288 Chamberlin's *The Confessions of an Individualist*.
289 A combination would be Frederic William Wiles's
290 *News Is Where You Find It*. All serve a purpose,
291 obviously, and are vastly better reading than the
292 books of the last century because they are well organ-
293 ized, concise, and say something effectively.

294   Centuries hence, it is reasonable to believe, schol-
295 ars will turn as often to the reminiscences of journal-

[296] ists as to the recollections of statesmen in seeking to
[297] understand the first half of the twentieth century.

Analysis of the Article

The ultimate construction of this article followed the original plan for it, as is evident by study of its architecture. The deductive method was used. The piece opens on details (lines 1 to 11). Lines 12 to 19 suggest to the reader that he will be given the reasons for the literary change that is noted. Lines 20 to 34 document the assertion that anonymity once was the rule among journalists. From 34 to 109 the writer traces the practice by journalists of shedding their obscurity and modesty, naming and criticizing specific books by newspapermen and magazinists.

Lines 110 to 141 explain the new approach that was made to journalistic autobiography by Vincent Sheean; 142 to 160 show the effect of the Sheean method. Lines 161 to 181 discuss the work of still other journalists, both those who did and did not go on with the trend.

An attempt to account for this trend occupies lines 182 to 279; this section is almost totally analytical. With the next line begins broader criticism of the more recent autobiographies by journalists, ending at line 293. The final three lines offer a generalization that sums up the significance of the entire study made of these books and their authors.

Another Way to Build Articles

Some writers have such retentive memories or photographic minds that they can construct an article in their heads and simply pour it out on paper, more or less ready-made. Usually this can be done most effectively with a piece around one thousand or fifteen hundred words long; for any extraordinary length it takes the mind of a mental giant like that of the English historian, Lord Macaulay, who is said once to have recited *Paradise Lost* after one reading. He did so to distract seasick travelers crossing the English Channel.

Bernard De Voto, author of innumerable critical articles for *The Saturday Review, Harper's* and other periodicals, once told

Robeson Bailey, a teacher of article writing, that he rewrote constantly. ". . . not even the briefest editorial that had been completely shaped in his mind before he sat down to write it was allowed to go to the printer until it had been through the typewriter—that means rewritten—at least three times."

Robert C. Marsh, music critic of the Chicago *Sun-Times,* a contributing editor of *High Fidelity* magazine, author of a widely read biography of Arturo Toscanini, and a former member of the University of Chicago faculty, has an extraordinary memory and an unusual ability to organize large bodies of material in his mind. "Almost everything I write I write in my head," he wrote the author of this book.

He was asked to describe precisely the background of an article on Toscanini that appeared in *High Fidelity.* Before the article is read, the author's tracing of its background and method of production should be studied. It soon will be evident that it was evolved in an entirely different manner than the article on "The Journalist as Autobiographer."

By Robert C. Marsh

In the autumn of 1953 I had just returned from a year in Europe and was about to begin a period of teaching as a visiting professor in the University of the State of New York. Before taking up my academic duties I drove to visit my father in Indiana, and on the journey back East I took the Pennsylvania Turnpike. I don't believe in radios in cars, chiefly because I find silence preferable to most daytime radio shows, so I faced the run from the Ohio line to Philadelphia with nothing much to occupy my thoughts. I was driving a Cadillac 60 Special that held the road the way a locomotive rides the rails, and with the manipulation of the car reduced to a few near-reflex actions, I had plenty of time for reflection.

I won't pretend that I can reconstruct the sequence of ideas that ran through my mind, but somewhere in the neighborhood of Pittsburgh I began to look forward to the fact that being near New York during the coming season I could hear Toscanini's broadcast concerts with the NBC Symphony at the source rather than via the long telephone wires that dimmed their fidelity in the Midwest. That led me to considering some of the Toscanini records I had heard in the weeks before, drawing me toward the conclusion that Toscanini, for someone who was difficult to record successfully, had actually made quite a number of things in recent years. Just how much of his repertory, I asked myself, had he actually put on disks? I was unable to answer this, so I stopped at Howard Johnson's and had a frankfort with mustard and other thought-producing additions, a milk shake, and a few moments of contemplation, uncomplicated by mechanical considerations.

When I got under way again the first thought that emerged from my digestive activity was that I had never seen a complete list of records by Toscanini. Of course I had seen listings, most of them the work of the RCA-Victor promotion department, but these omitted out-of-print disks, of which there were then quite a few, and otherwise failed to come up to my ideas of adequate discographic compilation. I wanted a complete list, and what's more I wanted one based on chronological order. That meant I had to know when (and it was only a short step to when and where) each of the records was made. This was another question I couldn't answer, but I assumed that RCA could, although I wasn't sure how to get them to do it. Faced with that puzzle I drove into the next Howard Johnson place and had a double chocolate something-or-other.

Buzzing on to Harrisburg I changed the subject and ran over the various explanations I had read for Toscanini's brilliance and mastery as a conductor. Most of them, I concluded, were unable to hold up under very close scrutiny, largely because they failed to hit on qualities which really distinguished between Toscanini and other musicians of justifiable reputation. However, I was convinced that the Maestro was a conductor of unique powers, and I got down to thinking about just what these were and why the descriptions I had read missed the mark.

It should be evident from all this that I have a disciplined power of recall concerning things which I have read, or given some attention to, so that—in a perfectly legitimate sense—I can claim to be able to do research in my head: i.e., review at will the materials I have read in an area of my interest. It ought to be stressed here, though, that my professorship was in the area of philosophy and the theory of education, subjects which had been my primary concern during the previous three or four years, and that although I usually read everything I could about Toscanini, I had really given him very slight attention during the months before this drive. I got to thinking about him largely as a relief from the subjects I had been working on, rather than as a continuation of an established line of inquiry.

By the time I reached Philadelphia I was convinced: (a) that I wanted to prepare a detailed discography of all the Toscanini recordings—the actual extent of which I did not then fully appreciate, I fear; (b) that this listing ought to contain evaluation—since I knew that some of the records were not good likenesses of the Maestro's music, and ought not to be so regarded by the future; (c) that this project should have appended to it an intellectually respectable analysis of the Maestro's musicianship.

As the reader who knows my series of articles in *High Fidelity* or their expanded version in *Toscanini and the Art of Orchestral Performance* will appreciate, I had already formulated the central portion of what was to be a project that eventually took over a year of my time and ended up as a book that has, to date, been published in three countries and two languages. Naturally, I had no idea that I was getting into such a job; as a matter of fact I ended the drive more or less convinced that someone other than myself was best suited to write the analytical essay I had in mind.

At the close of the day I made a few notes on a pad of paper about the piece and the way it ought to be written (I always carry a pad of paper with me), and that ended the matter for a week or so. When I was in

New York City, shortly after the start of the academic year, I had a short talk with a well-known critic who said he was busy with a book for an anxious publisher who was holding him to a strict set of deadlines, therefore the essay I suggested would be impossible for him. I tried someone else, and he wasn't interested in it, either. So I finally said to hell with all that and decided to write the piece myself. I began by going to RCA-Victor and asking them for help in getting the discographic information I needed. They were most courteous, and to my very great surprise supplied all the data I wanted—so I really had to do no research at all in securing the list of dates and places that made the discography so interesting to many readers.

As I indicate in the preface to the book, most of the material needed for the magazine piece (and the expanded version of the articles) could not be found in any library. The information I wanted had to be secured by finding people who knew Toscanini, preferably those who had played under him, engineers and others connected with his recording, and members of his family and immediate circle, etc., and getting them to discuss relevant matters with me. I can't say that I interviewed anyone for this express purpose; that is, the fact-gathering always was informal and cast in the form of asking questions in a conversational tone, and I usually made no notes until afterwards. (I very rarely make notes for any of my writing, having learned many years ago how to keep the information I need clear and well fixed until required.)

As I progressed finding the things I wanted to know, I made summaries of them on cards and slips of yellow paper, until about mid-way in the school year I decided that I ought to put a draft of this together, largely for the sake of clarification where the gaps were and what my approach was going to be. The greater part of the article was written in concentrated periods of an hour or so apiece during one week-end, working through small wads of notes I had clipped together because of a related theme, but not necessarily duplicating any of the notes, and frequently putting on paper for the first time long passages of analysis and interpretation which I had thought out carefully, sometimes weeks before, but had never bothered to write down previously.

With the manuscript in existence, I thought it was good enough to show to a publisher, so I sent it to John Conly at *High Fidelity*. He called me and said it was fine, could he have the discography? I sent that along a few weeks later; he bought the lot, and talking it over we decided that I should prepare the material as a three-part series for the magazine but continue on the larger scheme, which had now taken on unmistakable book proportions. That's what I did, but it's another story.

The illustrations used in *High Fidelity* were partly secured (by the magazine) from the Bettmann Archive, partly supplied by RCA (via myself). I might add, . . . that all an author has to do is get into a friendly working arrangement with skilled editors and an able production staff, such as *High Fidelity* can claim, and he need not worry about his work appearing in an attractive format. Of course, it's highly advantageous, since he can rest assured that they are as interested as he in presenting his work effectively, so all he has to do is worry about the writing—which, after all, is his main responsibility.

Some seven months after accepting this series I became Contributing Editor of *High Fidelity,* and (so far, anyway) we have been happy ever after. The final note on that score ought to be that I decided that I enjoyed writing about music more than I did teaching philosophy, so when the opportunity came along for me to become a full-time music critic on the Chicago *Sun-Times* I was delighted to take advantage of it.

The description above is complete, as to the mechanics of writing this article, but there is one further thing which must not be forgotten. A successful writer is almost certain to be a person who looks for significant experiences even in areas that are not his "official" concern and thus acquires resources on which he can draw when he needs them. I went into this Toscanini project with a backlog of more than ten years in which I gave Tos-

canini some degree of attention, not because I planned
to write a book about him, but because he interested me.
This provided a degree of assimilated familiarity which
no amount of intensive research could have duplicated,
I feel, at least in a short time. When I decided to write
this study, my jumping off place was a point well enough
along that my work always consisted in fitting details
into a pattern rather than building the framework from
scratch.

Mr. Marsh's article, later to become a chapter, with changes, in
his book on the great Italian orchestra conductor, was illustrated
with sketches and caricatures of Toscanini in mid-career; these
had added interest because they were by Enrico Caruso. The
article follows; after it comes a brief analysis of its construction.

By Robert Charles Marsh[3]

1   On December 18, 1920, Arturo Toscanini gath-
2   ered members of an Italian orchestra with which he
3   was touring the United States into a compact group
4   before the acoustical apparatus of the Victor Talk-
5   ing Machine Company in a Camden, New Jersey,
6   studio and made his first recordings: a minuet from
7   a Mozart symphony and a Respighi transcription of
8   a work by the father of Galileo.
9   Toscanini was at the mid-point of a long and re-
10   markable career. A man of 53, he had been conduct-
11   ing for 34 years; 34 more years were to pass before
12   he retired from the active direction of his last, and
13   probably finest, orchestra. Since the Nineties he had
14   been regarded as the foremost Italian conductor of
15   his time, and many were now hailing him as a musi-
16   cian of unequalled powers. Between that day and this,
17   some 225 Toscanini recordings have been made and
18   approved for release, giving the Maestro a recorded
19   repertory of about 160 works, roughly 70 of which

[3] Marsh, Robert Charles: "Toscanini on Records: 1920–1954." *High Fidelity*, December, 1954, pp. 40–42, 122. Reproduced by permission of both author and publisher.

20 exist in more than one version. (The champion in
21 this field is the Scherzo from Mendelssohn's *Mid-*
22 *summer Night's Dream* music: five different record-
23 ings.) Over 20,000,000 copies of Toscanini records
24 have been sold for more than $33,000,000, accord-
25 ing to RCA Victor sales-statisticians.

26   This is a listing and evaluation of his records, a
27 preliminary appraisal of the documents in sound
28 which Toscanini has left for the generations who will
29 never hear him in a concert hall and who will have
30 to rely upon recordings to understand the principles
31 of honesty-in-musicianship for which he always stood
32 and to appreciate his contribution to the art of or-
33 chestra performance.

34   Recording is not a new thing, but faithful repro-
35 duction of anything as complex as the sound of a
36 symphony orchestra is a recent phenomenon. The
37 acoustical method was adequate for preserving human
38 voices; recordings of singers made even 50 years ago
39 give a reasonably accurate impression of the artist.
40 Pre-electrical recordings of symphony orchestras, on
41 the other hand, are poor as a group; and although
42 some early electrical recordings have life in them in
43 spite of limited fidelity, really faithful reproduction
44 of orchestral sound is less than 20 years old. Now, if
45 one were to document phonographically the 68 years
46 of Toscanini's career, it would be necessary first to
47 have adequate disks from his early period, and then
48 to have widely spaced re-recordings of a number of
49 works so that major changes in his manner of per-
50 formance could be noted. The recordings necessary
51 for such documentation do not exist, although ace-
52 tates of NBC Symphony broadcasts, air-check re-
53 cordings of his broadcasts with the Philharmonic-
54 Symphony of New York, and similar materials ex-
55 tend the available recordings far beyond the list of
56 commercially released disks given here. Unfortu-
57 nately, technicalities prevent the circulation of re-
58 cordings of broadcasts, rehearsals, etc., even for study
59 purposes. One hopes, however, that in time some

⁶⁰ of this additional Toscanini material will be avail-
⁶¹ able to students in the form of society issues or on
⁶² some other restricted basis.

⁶³ For half of his career Toscanini made no records.
⁶⁴ In middle life we have a brief acoustical series from
⁶⁵ 1920/21 and early electrical recordings from 1926
⁶⁶ and 1929. At 69, Toscanini made the great 1936
⁶⁷ series with the Philharmonic-Symphony Orchestra of
⁶⁸ New York, and from that date to the present there
⁶⁹ have been recording sessions at frequent intervals,
⁷⁰ though there have been some seasons in which Tos-
⁷¹ canini made no records. It is the septuagenarian
⁷² Maestro who began to record liberally after 1937,
⁷³ and it is the octogenarian Toscanini who comes to
⁷⁴ us with high fidelity. He has said in the past that he
⁷⁵ would conduct until he is 90, and I feel that if he
⁷⁶ wishes he can fulfill this promise. Although he no
⁷⁷ longer wants to be committed for a winter season, I
⁷⁸ do not think that the last Toscanini concert or re-
⁷⁹ cording session has taken place. Nonetheless, what
⁸⁰ we have on modern disks comes from the final
⁸¹ decades of a very long career. Toscanini the musician
⁸² has been before the public and the critics since 1886;
⁸³ the high fidelity recordings are the work of the Old
⁸⁴ Man.

⁸⁵ Toscanini has always viewed making records as an
⁸⁶ ordeal, and until fairly recently he was not especially
⁸⁷ interested in putting his performances on disks. The
⁸⁸ drastic reduction of the relative levels of volume, the
⁸⁹ lack of presence, and the loss of tonal values, to-
⁹⁰ gether with the general artificiality of recorded sound,
⁹¹ made it difficult for him to understand how one could
⁹² secure musical satisfaction from records. Coupled
⁹³ with this was his perfectionism and his demand that
⁹⁴ no record should be released without his approval.
⁹⁵ This made a Toscanini recording session something
⁹⁶ of a nightmare. On 78 rpm a single slip could ruin a
⁹⁷ side—four minutes of tense, and otherwise perfect,
⁹⁸ work. A series of slips could result in his rejection
⁹⁹ of an entire album. One factor in the increase of

¹⁰⁰ Toscanini recordings in recent years has been the
¹⁰¹ introduction of tape recording and the resultant ease
¹⁰² in editing masters.

¹⁰³ The most celebrated instance of a long and ex-
¹⁰⁴ pensive series of recording sessions producing noth-
¹⁰⁵ ing at all for commercial release was Toscanini's 1942
¹⁰⁶ series with the Philadelphia Orchestra, when the
¹⁰⁷ *Pathétique, La Mer, Death and Transfiguration,* the
¹⁰⁸ Schubert Ninth and Berlioz's *Queen Mab Scherzo*
¹⁰⁹ were recorded. Technically the performances had
¹¹⁰ minor flaws, though some were approved, but the re-
¹¹¹ cording was at too low a level to permit correction by
¹¹² dubbing, and in some instances no second masters
¹¹³ were cut; so when in a tragic accident the masters
¹¹⁴ were damaged in the electroplating process, the whole
¹¹⁵ series became an almost total loss, so far as concerns
¹¹⁶ commercial release. Happily all these works have
¹¹⁷ been remade with the NBC Symphony, though not,
¹¹⁸ of course, with the Philadelphia's distinctive tone.

¹¹⁹ Early in the Forties, Walter Toscanini constructed
¹²⁰ a sound system for his father which made use of 16
¹²¹ speakers wired in parallel and mounted in groups of
¹²² four. This provided a sense of non-directional sound
¹²³ emerging from a wide source, and with adequate vol-
¹²⁴ ume the Maestro was able to secure some feeling
¹²⁵ of orchestral presence. Since then the household's
¹²⁶ audio furnishings have changed and multiplied vastly.
¹²⁷ Walter Toscanini now presides over a very well
¹²⁸ equipped sound laboratory in what was once a bil-
¹²⁹ liards room. The Maestro's studio is fitted with a
¹³⁰ coaxial speaker in a folded-horn enclosure; in his
¹³¹ enormous living room he listens to an Altec 820-A,
¹³² fed by a 90-watt custom-built amplifier in the labora-
¹³³ tory. The increase in the number of recordings he has
¹³⁴ made in recent seasons can be attributed in part to
¹³⁵ his realization of advances in recording techniques.

¹³⁶ A great deal has been written to explain the unique
¹³⁷ qualities in Toscanini's musicianship. Such ex-
¹³⁸ planation is difficult, and since simple, misleading
¹³⁹ answers are easier to give than complex, accurate

¹⁴⁰ ones, a great many naive or incorrect statements have
¹⁴¹ been made. We are told, for example, that the impact
¹⁴² of a Toscanini performance derives from absolute
¹⁴³ fidelity to the score. This, certainly, is misleading; for
¹⁴⁴ though Toscanini is scrupulous in making no unwar-
¹⁴⁵ ranted changes in the music and has come to loathe
¹⁴⁶ the word "interpretation" and what is done in its
¹⁴⁷ name, he does deviate from the printed music. Un-
¹⁴⁸ like a Stock, he does not add extra bars to a Schu-
¹⁴⁹ mann symphony or an organ to Chausson's, and
¹⁵⁰ unlike a Stokowski he does not subject Wagner to
¹⁵¹ "symphonic synthesis" or eliminate the coda to
¹⁵² Tchaikovsky's *Romeo and Juliet*. But he does make
¹⁵³ changes. I have looked at some of the scores on his
¹⁵⁴ shelves and they are full of the sort of markings that
¹⁵⁵ one would expect to find in a scholar's library: cor-
¹⁵⁶ rections of printer's errors; inconsistencies in the
¹⁵⁷ composer's notation, and (most important) mistakes
¹⁵⁸ in the composer's calculation, such as bad disposition
¹⁵⁹ of parts which obscures harmonic progression or
¹⁶⁰ which buries melodic lines under the texture of the
¹⁶¹ orchestration. If Brahms gives the horn a low note
¹⁶² that does not sound well, Toscanini reserves the right
¹⁶³ to cut it out, and in this he is merely fulfilling his
¹⁶⁴ duties as a conductor.
¹⁶⁵   In eighteenth-century works the printed score often
¹⁶⁶ gives incomplete instructions as to the details of per-
¹⁶⁷ formance, particularly with respect to dynamics, and
¹⁶⁸ here careful study and editing of the parts is a neces-
¹⁶⁹ sary responsibility of a conductor. Toscanini is a fine
¹⁷⁰ enough scholar to do this extremely well, while Kous-
¹⁷¹ sevitzky, for instance, was notoriously weak along
¹⁷² these lines. Toscanini's wonderful performance of
¹⁷³ *La Mer* is due partly to the painstaking manner in
¹⁷⁴ which he has edited the score, doubling the parts to
¹⁷⁵ make them sound, when he felt the original orches-
¹⁷⁶ tration was too light, and adjusting the dynamics so
¹⁷⁷ that every line of the instrumentation could be heard.
¹⁷⁸ For these changes he went to Debussy seeking per-
¹⁷⁹ mission, which was granted. However, it is not this

180 fidelity or musical scholarship of itself that accounts
181 for Toscanini's excellence as a conductor, since he
182 shares these qualities with musicians of lesser stature.
183   We are told that Toscanini is a master of the or-
184 chestra, that he is familiar with the technique of all
185 the instruments, and that with years of experience
186 to draw upon he should be expected to use their
187 resources to maximum effect. This, too, is true but
188 incomplete. Many conductors are thoroughly familiar
189 with the resources of the orchestra and can produce
190 effects which, as effects go, are just as spectacular
191 as those Toscanini can command. The Boston Sym-
192 phony under Koussevitzky and the Philadelphia Or-
193 chestra under Stokowski were both just as fabulously
194 beautiful as any orchestra under Toscanini. One can
195 agree, then, that Toscanini knows the orchestra for-
196 ward and backward, but this is not the reason for his
197 primacy among conductors.
198   The same must be said of his supposedly unique
199 evocative power. He is a splendid disciplinarian,
200 as are many other conductors; more than this, he
201 can get men to share his intensity and give them-
202 selves to the music without holding any feeling or
203 emotional energy in reserve. This is a rare quality,
204 but I do not think that Toscanini is the only con-
205 ductor of our day to possess it, and it is not the thing
206 that sets him apart from his contemporaries.
207   Another explanation tells us that Toscanini is the
208 master of styles, that he always plays music in the
209 idiom best suited to it, thereby stating it in the most
210 effective manner. This is another partial truth. Tos-
211 canini is really the master of only one style, his own,
212 but this is based so securely on what seem to be
213 fundamental principles of good musical performance
214 (for example, that the ensemble should be so bal-
215 anced that every line of the orchestration can be
216 heard) that it is virtually a universal style and right
217 for everything. Persons who make an issue of style
218 usually mean by this the traditional manner in which
219 works are played, and in this sense Toscanini rejects

²²⁰ style completely. He spurns the distortions and senti-
²²¹ mentality that usually go with Tchaikovsky, the
²²² Romberg approach to Schubert, the muddy sounds
²²³ that are supposed to capture the spirit of Brahms,
²²⁴ and the emasculating "Viennese" mannerisms that
²²⁵ are inflicted upon Beethoven. The Toscanini style is
²²⁶ based upon years of analytic study of scores with the
²²⁷ determination to play them honestly and effectively.
²²⁸   There are other generalizations that are equally
²²⁹ faulty: that Toscanini's tempi are always faster than
²³⁰ what is usual for the work, that they never vary from
²³¹ one performance to another, that they are always
²³² metronomically exact. Certainly, Toscanini's sense
²³³ of tempo is extraordinarily keen, but his tempi in
²³⁴ a given work do change from one performance to
²³⁵ the next, and over the years his performances of
²³⁶ some works have altered a good deal. He has played
²³⁷ a Brahms symphony one way in the spring and an-
²³⁸ other way in the following autumn. Some works he
²³⁹ has speeded up and others he has slowed down.
²⁴⁰ Similarly, though some of his performances are
²⁴¹ markedly faster than those of other conductors, some
²⁴² are also slower. The fact is that in these things Tos-
²⁴³ canini is no different from many of his contempo-
²⁴⁴ raries. His performances are living things, produced
²⁴⁵ from the heart and mind of an intense and percep-
²⁴⁶ tive musician, and it is inevitable that they should—
²⁴⁷ at different times and under different conditions—
²⁴⁸ change.
²⁴⁹   The truth of the matter, it seems to me, is that
²⁵⁰ Toscanini's unique qualities come from his under-
²⁵¹ standing of the nature of music and from a sense
²⁵² of dedication to an ethic of honest muscianship in
²⁵³ which it is not the great maestro but the great com-
²⁵⁴ poser who speaks through the orchestra. For him
²⁵⁵ the task of the conductor is to master the score and
²⁵⁶ combine intelligence with musical skill in giving voice
²⁵⁷ to what the composer has written. The gap between
²⁵⁸ Toscanini and the "interpreter-conductor," who places
²⁵⁹ himself above the composer and uses the music and

260 the orchestra as vehicles for the assertion of his will
261 and the enlargement of his ego, cannot be bridged;
262 and because so many conductors have allowed them-
263 selves to be affected in this way the selfless musician-
264 ship of Toscanini is alone sufficient to place him in
265 a category by himself.

266   It is not straining an analogy to speak of music as
267 a language. In a word-language used expressively,
268 as in poetry, we have the elements of the meaning
269 of words, accent, rhythm and tempo; the combination
270 of these things, as we read a poem, gives us our feel-
271 ing of coherence, continuity and form. A poem is an
272 artistic unity. If we change words, drop out or rear-
273 range lines, or read with accents other than those the
274 poet expected the words to have, we destroy the integ-
275 rity of the work and substitute an artless muddle. In
276 music the units are not words but combinations of
277 sounds, and just as any word cannot follow any
278 other word and still make sense, so certain combina-
279 tions of sounds have a significance when followed
280 by certain other combinations of sounds that they
281 would not otherwise possess. It is this fundamental
282 thing about tonality, certain sounds seeming to lead
283 naturally into other sounds, that gives us a basis for
284 harmony and that allows the creation of feelings of
285 tension and repose which, in a rhythmic pattern, are
286 the fundamentals of musical structure.

287   The basis of a Toscanini performance is the
288 rhythmic pattern he has selected as best fitted to the
289 expressive content of the music. This rhythmic
290 foundation does not change in the work except when
291 the composer has indicated that it should. There is
292 consequently a line to the performance, a steady pro-
293 pulsive force which is always felt and which is never
294 sacrificed to a special effect, but is always present and
295 gives the work coherence and cumulative power. The
296 wonderful plastic qualities of Toscanini performances
297 come from the fact that within this rhythmic pattern
298 he can pass from the softest to the loudest dynamic
299 levels and through a score of changes in expression

300 or orchestral color without losing the integral drive
301 of the harmonic rhythm. The nature of a work of
302 music is that it must be revealed as a sequence in
303 time, but the composer and the conductor must see
304 it as a structural unity in which all parts are properly
305 balanced in terms of the entire composition. The
306 unique quality of Toscanini performances comes, es-
307 sentially, from his magnificent sense of form.
308   In recent years that sense has caused him to elimi-
309 nate the most elementary of rhetorical devices. We
310 are all familiar with the habit of slowing up on con-
311 cluding chords, so that they come *dah* DUM *dah*
312 (say). Toscanini once did this to a limited degree, but
313 today he has eliminated nearly all rhetorical expres-
314 sion from his playing, and this is probably the greatest
315 contrast between his conducting and that of German
316 musicians. Those who say they don't like Toscanini
317 are probably saying that they don't like the absence
318 of rhetoric; but after one senses the greater intensity
319 of Toscanini's "singing style" most rhetoric seems
320 crude and tasteless.
321   Let us contrast Toscanini with his *bête noire,* Furt-
322 wängler. The Furtwängler method is to allow the mu-
323 sic to fall naturally into phrases and groups of phrases,
324 and these simple statements are spun out to the
325 length of the work. In music for which Furtwängler
326 has special affinity, such a performance can be elo-
327 quent, moving and beautiful, though lacking in inten-
328 sity, cohesion and cumulative power. In works for
329 which Furtwängler has no special affinity, or in which
330 he wishes to make a great effect, this method must
331 be modified, and since there is no line giving unity
332 to the performance, the only way that excitement can
333 be produced is by acceleration and retardation for
334 emphasis. In this way the composition becomes a
335 series of episodes in sequence, and the form and the
336 artistic unity of the work may be lost.
337   The defects of Furtwängler are those of taste and
338 musical understanding, while the faults of a Toscanini
339 come from characteristics desirable in the mean being

340 carried to excess. His rhythmic accuracy is splendid,
341 but at times he is metronomic, the music having
342 mechanical precision but no feeling. His intensity is
343 magnificent, but there are times when he is too in-
344 tense and the music loses power and eloquence by
345 being so hard driven that it cannot sing and reveal its
346 content fully. Happily, Toscanini has a sound sense
347 of the mean and it is usually observed.
348   Toscanini does not like to be called a great con-
349 ductor. "I am no genius," he has been quoted as say-
350 ing repeatedly. Rather than protest, let us take him at
351 his word. I, for one, have had enough of genius
352 conductors who feel free to tamper with the music
353 of genius composers. Let us have honesty, dedication
354 and musicianship.

Analysis of the Article

The editor of *High Fidelity* published the discography separately from this article, and in several parts. The construction
of the main article is clear.

It goes from the particular to the general (lines 1 to 25). The
third paragraph sets forth the article's purpose. From lines 34 to
62 we find general background on recording of music. From lines
63 to 135 Mr. Marsh discusses Toscanini's recording sessions,
methods, and results. He then (lines 136 to 320) takes up, in what
constitutes the heart of the article, certain critical generalizations
about Toscanini's musicianship, analyzing these, declaring them
fallacious, and giving his personal reactions. He next (lines 321
to 347) indulges in some authoritarian criticism by contrasting
Toscanini with Furtwängler. He concludes (lines 348 to 354) on
a generalization about conductors.

Writing Syndicated Criticism

Rare is the journalistic writer who has not dreamed that what he has to say will someday be read beyond the boundaries of the one newspaper or magazine in which his work appears. Critical writers are no exception to the yen for syndication of views and ideas.

This ambition is particularly true of the newspaper critic, for his publication is distributed only locally. The United States has no national newspapers in the sense that geographically smaller countries possess them, as for instance England, where the Manchester *Guardian* or any of the London dailies can reach all corners of the island in time for reading at breakfast. Newspaper critics often feel alone and actually are isolated, because their writings are seen almost solely by the readers in their geographical or subject areas. These readers do include, however, the people in publishing or production offices who keep track of reviews, authors and artists who employ clipping services, and a few readers in libraries.

Take, for instance, critics like Milton R. Bass, of the Pittsfield (Mass.) *Berkshire Eagle*, which has a circulation of not quite 30,000. Mr. Bass writes a general column twice weekly called "The Lively Arts" and a book column for Saturdays, and reviews television, movies, radio, music, recordings, and occasionally painting and sculpture. He arranges for other book reviewers to submit copy, edits special pages, assigns music reviews during the heavy summer season. Mr. Bass' work is worthy of wider reading; his versatility has been explained earlier.

Critics for magazines with circulations not much larger than newspapers, for instance, are assured of somewhat wider reading and consequently more national attention. Robert Hatch, books and arts editor of *The Nation,* whose circulation is numerically similar to that of the *Berkshire Eagle,* is read in every state of the union and in many foreign countries, since his magazine is subscribed to widely if not largely. B. H. Haggin, music reviewer for *The New Republic,* also can count on being read widely even though his periodical has a much smaller distribution than, say, the Albany *Knickerbocker News* (27,496 for *The New Republic* and 54,000 for the *Knickerbocker News*).

Magazine readers interested in evaluation of the arts select periodicals that publish the writings of particular critics they desire to follow. If Winthrop Sargeant should move from *The New Yorker* to *The Reporter* it is likely that a number of his loyal readers would go with him to the other magazine.

Nevertheless even magazine critics are not necessarily satisfied with the reader group they possess, and certainly the newspaper critic yearns to extend his circle of influence. The syndicate provides a convenient method for doing so.

Syndicates are companies that make a business of distributing various types of copy—news, interpretative articles, criticism, features, short stories, cartoons, comic strips, and virtually any type of material that appears in print—to noncompeting publications simultaneously.

Multiple distribution of this sort is now more than a century old in the United States. In elementary form it has been traced back to the old New York *Sun,* which in 1841 sold extra copies of President John Tyler's message to Congress to other newspapers to cut down its own and their costs. This principle has developed until today there are almost two hundred different firms that distribute various types of material, including book reviews, radio and television criticism, and evaluations of all the other arts except architecture, although as already noted in an earlier chapter, regular dissemination of criticism is less common than is news coverage of the arts.

Syndicated criticism is produced most commonly in two ways: Under one plan regular criticism by staff writers is made available to other newspapers. Thus Don Freeman's television reviews for the San Diego *Union* are syndicated to the other papers in the Copley chain via the Copley News Syndicate. Through another plan, critics not attached to any particular publication write for the syndicate. John Barkham, for example, writes book reviews for *The Saturday Review* syndicate. They do not appear in the magazine itself and he is not on the magazine's staff.

A Syndicate Described

The Saturday Review, the influential weekly magazine of literature and public affairs and several other arts that began as a magazine devoted to literature only, runs as an auxiliary a syndicated service of criticisms of both books and music. Known as "Book Service for Newspapers" and "Music Service for Magazines," this includes duplicated copy on legal-size sheets and glossy photographs or mats of the authors of books or the musicians under discussion.

A typical book release from this syndicate includes a 600-word review of the volume considered worthy of the "Lead Review of the Week," often with a photograph or a mat. This generally is written by Harrison Smith, president of *The Saturday Review*. This is followed by a regular article, running from 800 to 1,200 words, called "Books Readers Liked Best," based on "A continuing survey . . . among readers of *The Saturday Review* to ascertain what books they are reading and which they like best. . . ." From four to six slightly shorter reviews, 300 to 500 words apiece, also are included, as well as "Book Notes," devoting from 200 to 300 words to reviews of another half-dozen books. Next comes a series of one- or two-paragraph bits of news called "Among Books and Authors," reporting on current events related to books, progress of volumes being written, and the like. The next take is a page of one-paragraph reviews of "Books for Young People," and the last is a page telling editors what books are to be reviewed in future releases.

The music release is less elaborate. It begins usually with a signed general article of around 1,000 words on developments, personalities, or news of the music world called "The Music Box." The same author (Irving Kolodin, *The Saturday Review* music editor and author of books on music) writes 500 or 600 words on the "Personality of the Week." Sometimes there also is a review of some outstanding musical event, running a page or two of copy. Photographs or mats frequently are included. The rest of the release consists of a page of one- or two-sentence reviews of the latest records, divided into classical and popular.

These releases go out weekly; in 1958 about 75 papers were purchasing them and printing them either as a major Sunday feature, selecting different segments as a daily feature, or using segments on Sundays only.

William D. Patterson, associate publisher of *The Saturday Review* and manager of this syndicate, explained in a letter to the author that "It has been our theory that newspapers would welcome a service which would help them strengthen their cultural coverage without involving them in heavy, specialized staff expense. Our theory has been rewarded by the number of papers now using the services and by regular inquiries from others who are interested. . . ."

As already stated, the copy is written especially for these releases and has not appeared previously in the magazine, nor is it used by the magazine later. This, in effect, provides a considerable separate activity for the writers, notably Mr. Kolodin.

The effect of such a syndicate is, of course, to discourage home talent. For a number of years one of the Sunday morning newspapers in Syracuse, N. Y., ran original reviews by its Sunday editor. After his death these were replaced by *The Saturday Review* syndicate materials. Other effects are possibly to increase the quality of the reviewing but also to standardize the criticism. The dangers of this standardization are well put by Prof. Robert W. Root, in his chapter on syndicates in *Journalism Tomorrow*, a symposium on journalism. He wrote:

"We have syndicated book reviews and syndicated TV criticisms. Soon, if they have not already, syndicates will be offering predigested cultural opinions so that the reader in Phoenix as well as in Detroit will know what to think of a lately discovered Van Gogh or a new American symphony."

An Academic Variation

A variation on the commercial syndicate is a practice that has been followed for some years by the School of Journalism at the University of Missouri. This might suggest similar co-operation between other institutions of higher education and the press. Professor William Peden of the English department, who teaches the critical writing course for the journalism school and is a critic for the New York *Times Book Review* and other leading publications, obtains review copies of books from publishers and builds the practical phase of his course on the reviewing by students of books and other art forms.

These reviews are published in the *Columbia Missourian,* a daily produced by students and staff of the journalism school for the city of Columbia, seat of the university. From a dozen to fifteen of these reviews are reprinted in a clipsheet and offered without charge, in a biweekly release, to newspaper editors anywhere. Begun in 1952, this system is now placing book criticisms in more than one hundred dailies and weeklies, mostly in the Missouri area, but some in distant states. No changes are made in the original copy for syndication purposes.

The Writing Angle

Writers for syndicates declare that their work, so far as reviewing and criticism are concerned, is done in about the same way as for local consumption. Mr. Patterson explained: "I suppose the only real difference in our approach to syndicate coverage is that we have to write a little more briefly and that we are probably a bit more aware of a broader, more popular readership. There are no significant differences in the form or viewpoint otherwise."

Naturally the critic who syndicates his material must avoid

references that are mysteriously regional. His references must be broad and his topics of universal interest if they are to achieve maximum readership outside the local territory. His vocabulary must not be too strongly colloquial if it is to be understood thousands of miles away. As any journalist constantly tries to write to the interests and experience of his readers, so the syndicated critic seeks to project himself into the frame of reference of his readers. His approach to his subject is likely to be national or international rather than regional. He attempts to acquaint his reader with incidents, names, and titles, so that they are in rapport. A television reviewer can assume general knowledge of the prominent comedians and masters of ceremonies, but he has to explain and justify his inclusion of someone on a local station who is only a home-town celebrity.

Syndicated critical copy is prepared as is any other, allowing only for the differences in scope, style, and approach already mentioned. Instead of being given to a city or news desk in a newspaper office or to a certain associate editor of a magazine, it is turned over to the person on the syndicate staff responsible for copy-editing it and seeing it through the duplicating or printing machines. Since much syndicated criticism is actually based on earlier use in a publication, it may not be seen by its author after it has left his hands for local use, unless he is connected with one of the few magazines that sends proofs to its writers.

The writer whose copy is distributed by one of the news services (Associated Press or United Press International to name the largest of all) prepares his material in the same way as do the other writers for the news agency. In any case it is given a scanning by a desk, cut to fit the budget of copy being transmitted to member or client publications, and put on the wire like any news copy. About the only difference for the news-service writer is in the timing. He has fewer opportunities to cover opening nights of plays or first showings of other arts. Even the most widely known of such events, like the debut of the Metropolitan Opera season in New York, is covered as news rather than criticized. What little criticism goes over the wires is long-range, approaching the critical article rather than the review in character. Parts of the copy are prepared in advance, such as side-bar stories (interviews with stars, biographical sketches, historical articles), so they can be sent when the wires are not crowded with spot news material. What has been said in this paragraph applies also to the criticism contained in the budgets of the news services that send material for radio and television news and feature program use.

Examples of Syndicated Criticism

Because book publishers, for instance, distribute review copies as much as a month ahead of publication, writers for syndicates have ample time to prepare their material for release on a date coinciding with a book's appearance on the sales table. (Here is an instance of the commercial impact of publishing on criticism. Artistically there is no relationship between what the critic thinks of the book and when it is published; if he times his review to help the sale of the book he is a promotion man as well as a critic.) Reviewers of motion pictures, plays, and television shows similarly are able to get an advance look at what is to be exposed to the public officially at some later date by attending rehearsals or previews.

Here are examples of criticism as distributed by three types of syndicates: a book and music service connected with a national magazine, a wire service that comments on many different art forms, and a syndicate confined to television reviews.

The first, a book review, begins in the authoritarian manner of using other novels on World War II as a basis for establishing the nature of the new one. Most of the review is descriptive rather than critical, but there are enough critical touches ("a remarkable gift for creating characters . . .") to indicate approval of the book.

THE UNDERGROUND CITY

By H. L. Humes. New York: Random House. 755 pp. $4.95.

Reviewed by Harrison Smith
President, *The Saturday Review*

There have been many novels written to tell the grim story of the greatest and most catastrophic conflict in

all history, the Second World War. Mr. H. L. Humes's
"The Underground City," in its complexity, its host of
characters, its visions of a harassed and bloody continent,
its transition from Armageddon to war's aftermath, is
unlike any other war novel this reader can recall. It is a
long book, a man's book, and it cannot be read hastily.
It does not embrace the entire war but the last months
of the military crisis when Normandy was invaded and
the American Army had landed on the beaches of Sicily
and Southern France. "Invasive war, Leviathan," he
writes in preface to one of his chapters, "came now from
the South . . . Swept on the roaring river of war and
events, submerged in headlong defeat, pell-mell in
thanksgiving and victory, in blood and the smell of death,
the strategies . . . of men were hourly reforged to
fit the fluid moment . . . Having untrammeled the
blood-crazy stallions, men were no longer masters, but
slaves to hope and catastrophe. . . ."

(*There follows an 8-line summary of the plot.*)

Mr. Humes has a remarkable gift for creating characters who live in the reader's memory.

(*These are described in the next 5 lines.*)

Though the picture of Paris, well named the Underground City, is fascinating, the war in the South is drama
at its highest pitch. The ferocity of the German retreat,
the ruthless slaughter of men, women and children in
small villages, the confusion of the savage ending of a
great war bring the novel to vivid life. It is complex and
obviously was designed to hold to the author's theme
in its various aspects. Not a book to be hastily read
through, it offers the reader "an embarrassment of riches"
if he has the patience to hold them in his mind.

—Saturday Review Syndicate. Reproduced
by permission of *The Saturday Review*

Irving Kolodin's article that follows is a brief one that con-
stituted part of his "The Music Box," and is entitled "Kurka's
Contribution to American Opera." It is a combination group re-

view, brief consideration of American opera in general, as an art expression, and evaluation of Robert Kurka's work in particular. Note how Mr. Kolodin mentions that "more exposure has been given to this subject [American opera] both at the Metropolitan and the New York City Center, on radio and TV, than at any time in the past two decades." By calling attention to these facts he hopes, apparently, to catch the interest of some distant reader who has seen or heard only the radio or television performance.

What is an American opera? At the end of a musical season in which more exposure has been given to this subject, both at the Metropolitan and the New York City Center, on radio and TV, than at any time in the past two decades, there should be some interesting observations to be made. Is it Barber's "Vanessa" or Douglas Moore's "Ballad of Baby Doe"? Is it the late Robert Kurka's "Good Soldier Schweik" or is it Vittorio Giannini's "Taming of the Shrew"?

The interesting observation about it all, it seems to me, is that it can be any of all of these things, or Carlisle Floyd's "Susannah" or Marc Blitzstein's "Regina." For the fact is that, being a highly various people, the art expressions we develop do not stem from a single tradition or background, but from as many different traditions or backgrounds as are represented in our racial origins. If the case were otherwise only subjects with an Indian background would be really American, and the generation which produced "Shanewis," "Natoma," and the like went all over that ground without finding a fertile spot.

My suspicion is that the question of "character" will eventually crystallize not around subject matter or idiom—Moore's "Baby Doe" is about as different in idiom from Floyd's "Susannah" as Verdi's "Aïda" is from Mascagni's "Cavalleria"—but around size, and what might be called performability. The scores, such as Barber's "Vanessa" or Giannini's "Taming of the Shrew," which aspire to acceptance by the world's international opera theaters, will be written for full-sized orchestra in the traditional way. The works of more modest expanse which can be performed in any ordinary theater (or by a college workshop) will tend to a more economical use of manpower, in the genre of "chamber opera" typified long ago by Richard Strauss's "Ariadne" and brought down to date by Britten's "Turn of the Screw" and, most recently, Kurka's "Good Soldier Schweik."

In this treatment of a character out of Jaroslav Hasek's novel (nominally related to World War I, but as basically contemporaneous as George Baker's Sad Sack or as classic as Prokofieff's Lt. Kije), Kurka has chosen to orchestrate his score for an ensemble of 18 woodwind and brass (plus percussion), thus giving him excellent means for satirizing military music. Dispensing with strings may seem a drastic approach to originality, but his well-varied effects only occasionally tend toward monotony. Moreover, though the wind writing is anything but simple, I imagine almost any well-trained college band could produce the personnel to play it, with sufficient rehearsal.

It is quite believable that, for another subject, Kurka might have chosen an ensemble of strings or a mixed group or perhaps even two pianos. The unfortunate fact is, however, that "The Good Soldier Schweik" must stand as the last as well as the most mature effort to his name, for the greatly talented Kurka succumbed to leukemia last December at the age of 35. But I suspect that his contemporaries, and other writers to come, will be studying "Schweik" closely to profit from Kurka's lead in showing one way how the problem of "performability" can be surmounted without sacrificing musical values.

William Ewald's review of a "This Is Your Life" television program is in marked contrast to the two preceding reviews in that it is vigorously critical and is marked by a number of highly original locutions ("not my cup of tears," "peering through a 21-inch keyhole every Wednesday," and "electronic feast"). Such a review is a denial that only local radio-television reviewers attack major programs and that trenchant criticism is confined to intellectual magazines like *The New Yorker* or *Partisan Review*. It should be noted, however, that the critic has selected a program widely viewed. It is reproduced here in the form in which it is received by newspapers via wire service.

NX26

(TELEVISION IN REVIEW)

BY WILLIAM EWALD

UNITED PRESS STAFF CORRESPONDENT

NEW YORK, FEB. 27.—(UP)—"THIS IS YOUR LIFE," AN ABC-TV SHOW, HAS WHAT I GUESS YOU COULD CALL A GHOULISH FASCINATION.

IT IS NOT MY CUP OF TEARS, BUT I CAN UNDERSTAND WHY SOME VIEWERS ENJOY IT—IT'S A LITTLE LIKE PEERING THROUGH A 21-INCH KEYHOLE EVERY WEDNES-DAY. BUT UNLIKE ORDINARY KEYHOLE PEERING, THERE'S NO SENSE OF GUILT INVOLVED BECAUSE EMCEE RALPH EDWARDS KEEPS ASSURING VIEWERS THAT IT'S ALL BEING DONE FOR GOOD REASONS—UPLIFT FOR THE VIEWER AND CARTHARSIS AND LOOT FOR THE VICTIM.

"THIS IS YOUR LIFE" FEEDS UPON THE CORPSES OF LIVES PAST AND EDWARDS MAKES THE MOST OF HIS ELECTRONIC FEAST, SALIVATING VERBALLY AS HE STICKS HIS KNIFE AND FORK INTO THE CARCASS AND STARTS CARVING.

LAST NIGHT'S SHOW WAS A TYPICAL EXAMPLE. THE TARGET WAS A RETICENT, SWEET-FACED WOMAN, MAR-THA MALLOY SMITH OF WATEROWN, MASS. LIKE MOST OF EDWARDS' VICTIMS SHE WAS LURED INTO POSITION BY WELL-INTENTIONED RELATIVES AND FRIENDS.

MRS. SMITH THOUGHT SHE WAS ATTENDING A TEACH-ERS CONFERENCE AND WHEN EDWARDS ANNOUNCED THAT THIS WAS TO BE HER LIFE, SHE SAT STUNNED, NOT MOVING. EDWARDS PROMPTLY BELLOWED IN HER EAR: "DON'T YOU KNOW WHAT'S GOING ON AROUND HERE? DIDN'T YOU HEAR WHAT I JUST SAID?"

MRS. SMITH WAS LED ON STAGE AND THE PARADE STARTED: HER BIG BROTHER, HER LITTLE BROTHER, HER

MOTHER, HER BROTHER-IN-LAW, HER 13-YEAR-OLD SON
AND A CONGEST OF ASSOCIATES WHO HAD ONCE FLOATED
AROUND THE FRINGES OF HER LIFE.

MRS. SMITH'S HUSBAND WASN'T THERE LAST NIGHT
AND THAT, OF COURSE, WAS EDWARDS' TWISTER AND THE
REASON FOR THE SHOW. AN AIRMAN, HER HUSBAND WAS
ONE OF THOSE KILLED IN JULY, 1945, WHEN AN ARMY
TRANSPORT PLOWED INTO THE EMPIRE STATE BUILDING.

EDWARDS MILKED THEIR COURTSHIP WHILE MRS.
SMITH BLINKED BACK TEARS AND HE MILKED SMITH'S
DEATH WHILE SHE SAT IN A STATE OF SEMI-COMA.

"AH," SAID EDWARDS IN SEPULCHRAL TONES, "TIME
HAS EASED THE PAIN FOR ALL OF YOU WHO SHARED IT
ON THAT DAY . . . SORROW, YES, BUT NOT DESPAIR . . ."

AND MRS. SMITH WEPT A LITTLE. AND A HAND FROM
ONE OF HER RELATIVES TOUCHED HER SHOULDER TO
STEADY HER.

WELL, THIS MAY BE ENTERTAINMENT, BUT I DOUBT IT.
IT SEEMS TO ME A TERRIBLE INVASION OF PRIVACY, A
CHEAP LURE-IN TO SELL A FEW LIPSTICKS.

IT'S ALL VERY WELL FOR EDWARDS TO EXPLOIT THOSE
WHO COURT PUBLICITY—SHOW BUSINESS FOLK, POLI-
TICIANS AND OTHER HEADLINE EATERS—BUT IT SEEMS
TO ME THAT IN STRETCHING AND PICKING AND PULLING
AT THE FABRIC OF JUST NICE PLAIN PEOPLE, HE IS
GUILTY OF SOMETHING VERY BASIC—A VIOLATION OF
DECENCY AND ORDINARY GOOD MANNERS.

—United Press International

The Previewers

Possibly the most influential critical writing in the area of television is that done for newspapers by firms that syndicate to
them brief reviews of network shows for advance publication.
The two leading services market their material under the names
T. V. Key and T. V. Scout.

The writers, as T. V. Key explains it, are a "staff of experts who
attend screenings, watch rehearsals, and analyze scripts in New
York and Hollywood." Gentle in tone, their reports also are likely
to be noncommittal, but are by no means always lacking in
discrimination. Here is a typical excerpt from the service:

"ANGEL IN THE AIR." (A repeat) A touching fable about a poor Southern woman who loses faith, and a traveling medicine man who gives it back to her, along with a worthless coin. Although the play runs out of steam before the finale, Janice Rule and Vincent Price (slightly restrained for a change) make it absorbing drama. 9 P.M. CBS.

—T. V. Key

Handling Special Pages and Sections

Robert L. Sokolsky, entertainment editor of the Syracuse (N. Y.) *Herald-Journal* and *Herald-American,* writes a daily television column and reviews all the new movies shown in that city of 235,000. He also is responsible for the editorial content of the radio-television and movie pages.

Bob Sokolsky's pages are typical in newspapers across the continent. His are the problems of all special page editors: last-minute advertising that pushes out or cuts into a cherished feature; inappropriate display advertising ("Is your child a needless victim of Bed-Wetting?"); and changes in radio and television programming or movie scheduling without adequate advance notice. Yet each day he is able to present useful and often attractive pages.

Special pages, more than special sections, are likely to be mélanges of copy. The few weeklies that run them, and many of the dailies, combine radio and television naturally enough, but they also allot space, at times, to reviews or news of forth-coming musical events, art shows, visits of ballet companies, and recitals by home-town artists. The special section, on the other hand, retains its purity because it is larger than a page and has more advertising potential.

The Place of Advertising

It should be clear at once that special pages and sections are made possible because they permit solicitation of advertising accounts that might otherwise not appear. A glance at any newspaper proves this, especially the bulging Sunday editions. Real-estate sections provide a natural locale for the advertising of realtors, builders, and others in related areas. Garden pages are sought out by green thumbers, so what is more natural than to find on them advertising for seeds, mowers, spades, and other supplies and tools?

A reviewer or critic can find no surer way to reach the public through newspapers and magazines than by convincing a publisher that he, the publisher, could get so many columns of advertising a year for a special page if he would give attention to the particular art form that fascinates the critic. But it is not enough for the journalist to go to the publisher and say that he *thinks* advertisers would rally to such a page. He first must go to the potential advertisers, sound them out, and get at least verbal commitment.

To the critic who is an aesthete this is a dirty business with which he wants no truck. To the critic who is a journalist it is a necessity that he understands and which is another sort of professional challenge. He knows that a publisher must pay for the composition of type, engraving of pictures, paper, ink, and other materials and labor that go into the publication of a single page. He knows, too, the practical fact that you cannot add one page only but must add two, since every sheet has two sides. Similarly, this practical man or woman knows that a given amount of advertising, usually of the display kind, is needed to underwrite the cost of producing a page. He has only two other arguments to add to that of advertising certainty. One is that such pages bring more readers to the whole paper, making the rest of the publication that much more effective as a medium of advertising and an influence in the community. The other is that the owners may wish to be identified with the world of the fine and popular arts, thereby performing a service for that world by publicizing and evaluating it.

Magazines are not much different from newspapers in this matter: attention to most of the arts has fluctuated sharply over the years in the history of both media. Criticism finds its place in popular magazines only if readers demand it, if editors and publishers are personally interested in it, or if critical journalists as well as aggressive advertising salesmen prove the revenue-earning values.

Special Page vs. Special Section

Separate special sections of newspapers actually are becoming more common in this country's journalism. Only three are devoted regularly to books, and none regularly to any of the other *fine* arts. But they run into the dozens on television and radio.

A special section of a paper, literally defined, means a tabloid supplement or a regular assembly of from six to a dozen or more eight-column pages all devoted to the same subject. Only the large metropolitan newspapers produce such separate journalistic entities regularly; smaller ones occasionally print one to mark a particular occasion, an occasion which will provide extraordinary amounts of advertising. Several dozen dailies issue magazines carrying the forthcoming week's radio and television log, with features, and, of course, ample advertising. These are distributed free as part of the paper. Many dozen others offer much the same material in tabloids of eight or more pages; as many more print such information, including critical material, on local programs and personalities, in separate sections. These are one of a half-dozen types, the others being on such topics as sports, society, women's interests, and finance. All these, with a few exceptions, are a regular part of the paper and cannot be bought independently, any more than one can buy the comics or one of the magazine sections, such as *This Week,* or *Parade,* separately from the rest of the paper.

The special page or pages, as differentiated from sections, are within a section devoted to other content, and are characteristic of daily, rather than Sunday, editions. Thus a large newspaper, provided it can sell enough advertising to support the venture, gives its readers a daily book page, a daily television-radio page, a daily motion picture-drama-music-ballet-recordings page, and sticks the art critic's column in one or the other depending upon the exigencies of make-up.

Special sections of magazines are common, but none constitutes a completely separate unit. There is a physical reason for this that does not hold with newspapers. A tabloid supplement or an eight- or twelve-page section of a newspaper can be folded into the paper, which is unbound. But magazines are bound. A separate, loose section would become a second magazine. Sections are dressed, therefore, to appear like magazines within magazines. Among the literary, art, idea, scholarly, and other periodicals, it is not uncommon to find occasional and even regular parts devoted to one or more of the arts. An example is the "SR/Recordings Section" included once monthly in the weekly *Saturday Review.*

Typical Pages

Bob Sokolsky's radio-TV or movie page is typical, containing many of the ingredients of all such pages. Here they are for his radio-television page:

"Looking and Listening," his signed column on radio and television, headed also by a thumbnail of a happy-looking critic.

"TV Best Bets," previews of certain net work shows obtained from a syndicate.

"TV Previews," one-paragraph summaries of programs to be seen or heard locally, and not covered by the syndicate; some are of home-town origin.

"Television" and "Radio Timetable," the logs.

"Radio Highlights," a few paragraphs pointing up certain programs.

From two to five engravings, usually one-column head pictures of TV performers who are to be visible on the day's programs.

Occasional features, especially on Sundays, by syndicated television feature writers and critics. An article on the use of animals in TV productions: "This Jungle Series Is Tough on Cobras."

The chinks are filled with shorts of from one to five paragraphs, bearing such important tidings as "Barry Nelson Returns to TV" or just "New Western."

Producing the Page

We have seen what is on a typical special page. How does it get there? The production line is precisely that followed by any other page. The advertising department contracts for the paid

BOOKS · MUSIC · and ART · NEWS and REVIEW

BY EUGENE B. SLOAN

Sumter Little Theatre Names New Officers

Bookmobile Schedule

Best Sellers
(According To Publishers' Weekly)

Stage Society Will Meet Monday Night

Portrait of Andrew Jackson which will go on exhibit today at Columbia Art Museum.

AT ART MUSEUM
Fine Jackson Portrait Goes on Exhibit Today

C. SLOAN
IN WASHINGTON

Opening Set For Musical By Columbian

Famed Passion Play Slated at Hendersonville

OUTDOOR STORIES
Dogs, Bass, Quail and Chiggers Star in Dr. Babcock's New Book

DR. HAVILAH BABCOCK

Dr. Babcock Writes When Mood Hits Him

By BOB TALBERT

HE'S A PERFECTIONIST
Recording Session Proves Long, Drawn-Out Affair for Van Cliburn

By HUGH A. MULLIGAN

Book Details Events Leading To Ft. Sumter

Mixed Children

Not Enough History

PLAN OPEN HOUSE: Members of the Players' Club prepare for the Town Theatre Open House which will be held Monday.

ADLESS BOOK-MUSIC-ART PAGE (Columbia State)

ART-MUSIC-THEATER PAGE (*Christian Science Monitor*)

The Book Corner

★ ★ ★

Faith Brought Him Through War's Peril

THE HOUR HAD COME. By Go Poto Seng, Dmitro Publications 220 pages.
By FREDERIC S. MARQUARDT

Author Dislikes Gertrude Stein

ART BY SUBTRACTION: A Dissenting Opinion of Gertrude Stein. By B. L. Reid, University of Oklahoma Pr.

Last Week's Best Sellers

FICTION

NONFICTION

Koehler Gets Bang Out Of Job

Why Ladd Has Store

NOVELIST — Eileen

FUN!

'Self-Portrait In Costume'
By George De Chitten

Art Exhibitions Around The Valley

Her Father No Help

Ione Robinson's Book To Tell Of Artistic Confusion Abroad

By ANSON B. CUTTS

BOOK AND ART PAGE (Phoenix *Arizona Republic*)

time limitations, even though the special page copy for an afternoon daily is largely set up the previous day. On magazines more care is exercised, for there is time to be more watchful. Also, what is not used in one issue cannot be published in the next, for issues may be a month or three months apart, not a single day, as on a newspaper.

Galley proofs are read, the page is made up in one of several ways (roughly sketched on a miniature blank page of the paper; right at the stone from a picture in the editor's mind; from a schedule or list in the hands of a printer; or from a dummy consisting of the proofs trimmed and pasted into their designated positions). The page proofs are read in turn, missing lines supplied, such as picture credits, and last-minute changes and other improvements are requested. When all have been made, the page is locked and is ready to roll.

It appears to one who looks over a large number of special pages in newspapers that only on the largest publications[1] is extra effort exerted to give variety to these pages. Like so much in American journalism, the daily special page is reduced to a routine in the interest of speed of production. This becomes a necessity when an editor seeks to avoid unnecessary type composition and also must put the page together on the fringe of his time.

How time-consuming the work of handling such a page can be is illustrated by one item for a book page: the best-seller list. A community may have only four bookstores. But these must be called up regularly and their reports combined and typed into lists possibly divided into fiction, nonfiction, and children's books. Titles and authors' names must be verified. This may seem like a small job, but a literary editor-critic who, as is common, also must devote time to other parts of the paper can find it an onerous chore.

[1] The New York *Times* Sunday edition includes an entire section, usually of 24 pages, in which at least one page of reading matter apiece is devoted to drama, motion pictures, music, art, television, recordings, radio, the dance, and photography (gardening, home improvement, stamps and coins also occupy space). This practice is exceptional and probably possible only in a metropolitan area like New York City.

If a special page is to hold readers and have some effect in the community, it must be reliable, constantly attractive, and well-organized typographically and in content. The *Christian Science Monitor*'s art-music-theater page each Saturday is an example of carefully produced work (see illustration).

Making the Page or Section Appealing

Writers on typography of the newspaper (little has been written on magazine typography) have explored the possibilities for making such special pages attractive and thereby increasing readership.[2]

Standard page make-up patterns are necessary in newspaper journalism to achieve speedy production. Magazine pages, however, do not follow fixed patterns because there are so many different sizes of magazines and therefore unlimited possibilities for make-up. The slower production pace of the magazine allows for experiment with unusual combinations of page elements.[3]

Content Elements of Pages

Based on the practices employed by editors of special pages in leading newspapers, the content elements of successful pages are clear. These elements take in two main types of material: advertising and reading matter. Advertising helps to finance a page but it rarely enhances its appearance (see the illustration of the adless page). All pages have certain ingredients in common, but there are enough differences to justify separate consideration. The critical journalist responsible for such a page at least gains from what follows an idea of the sort of material he might seek to use.

Few pages are devoted to art, music, or recordings alone, ex-

[2] See Allen, John E.: *Newspaper Designing;* Arnold, Edmund C.: *Functional Newspaper Design;* and Sutton, Albert A.: *Design and Makeup of the Newspaper.*

[3] The few magazine make-up references include: Butler, Kenneth, Likeness, George C., and Kordek, Stanley A.: *101 Usable Publication Layouts;* Ferguson, Rowena: *Editing the Small Magazine;* Price, Matlack: *Advertising and Editorial Layout.*

cept in unusual circumstances (such as special promotion in connection with a big convention or the opening of a new concert auditorium). Therefore only the financially practical or regularly appearing special pages are outlined here. Halftone and other types of engravings, it is assumed, will be used wherever possible.

Books

ADVERTISING—Bookshops, book departments of department stores, book publishers, writers' courses and conferences.

READING MATTER—Reviews, critical articles, best-seller lists, book news, critical column, literary features (syndicated), interviews with local authors, new books at libraries.

Art-Music-Drama-Dance-Recordings Combination Pages

ADVERTISING—Supply shops (painters' and sculptors' brushes, tools, etc., musical instruments), schools, conservatories, courses, music stores, concerts, recitals, plays (also other theatrical events), recordings and piano firms.

READING MATTER—Reviews, critical articles, personality sketches, human interest and historical features, news of local events.

Radio-Television

ADVERTISING—Network and local programs, supply houses, service and repair firms, technical schools, hearing aids, music stores and record shops.

READING MATTER—Radio and television logs, critical column, news columns and stories, advance reviews, high lights of radio and television programs.

Motion Pictures

ADVERTISING—Theaters.

READING MATTER—Reviews, editor's column, timetable of downtown movie houses, news, personality and other features, syndicated entertainment or amusement world columnists, features on trends in the industry or on the motion picture as an art form.

Editor's Dream

In his most pleasant dreams, the enthusiastic joint critic-editor sees himself responsible for an entire section or a group of pages on his subject. Few journalistic editor-critics, as we have seen, are given more space than a page a week. But it may be encouraging to know that the dream situations have a base in reality, and as the cultural explosion takes place, these may set a pace. It may be simultaneously discouraging and encouraging to look into such an office as that of the New York *Times Book Review*. The time may come when this generous treatment of books is extended to the arts other than literature; the principles already apply, after all, to the special section that covers at one time a half-dozen fine and popular arts (for example, the San Francisco *Chronicle*'s Sunday supplement)

Although not more than a half-dozen other newspapers are in a position to issue a publication at all comparable to the *Times Book Review*, certain of its practices could be duplicated on a smaller scale. It might be frustrating to some book editors to get a glimpse of the inside workings of the New York *Times* supplement, but it will inspire others and possibly give them a prod to use on their own publishers. To whatever extent other book editors learn from the best of the *Book Review*'s methods, their papers possibly could command something of the advertising and reader response that the *Book Review* has developed for itself.

Many a newspaper book editor or literary critic is cooped up in a small office or is restricted to a desk in a large, noisy room occupied by everything but literary pursuits. The *Book Review*, which is practically a separate magazine, has physical facilities the equal of a moderate-sized daily's entire editorial offices. A well-lighted room, measuring about 40' x 80' on the eighth floor of the *Times* building at 43rd Street and Seventh Avenue, houses the entire staff except the advertising salesmen. The editor has a private office, overflowing with books as might be imagined, but not in the disorder that such a flow suggests. The other staffers are in the main office, each with his own desk, some separated by tall bookcases or cabinets. One corner of the room holds a small reference library.

Founded in 1896, the *Book Review* by 1958 had achieved a circulation of 1,179,335, of which 10,491 copies were to individual subscribers. The remainder (1,168,844 copies) was distributed with the Sunday edition of the *Times*. Printed on an offset press, the supplement is prepared two weeks in advance of the regular paper, and sent out ahead of it for inserting later.

Most small dailies have an entire editorial and news staff not equal in size to that of the *Book Review*, which employs sixteen full-time writers, editors, and assistants as well as two secretaries. Among these editorial people are several widely known authors whose chief livelihood comes from their *Book Review* connection. Francis Brown, a biographer, is editor of the supplement. William DuBois, playwright, novelist, and critic, is fiction previewer. Lewis Nichols, columnist and feature writer, and J. Donald Adams, essayist and critic, both contribute departments. Two of the *Times'* most widely read critics, Orville Prescott and Charles Poore, are not in this list, because they run the book page of the daily edition, which has no connection with the *Book Review*.

Specimens of virtually the entire book production of the United States reach the offices of the publication, often two or three copies of each volume being sent. Of the approximately 10,000 received annually, about 3,000 are reviewed and a like number listed in "Other Books of the Week." Thus around 4,000 are neither reviewed nor mentioned, but, since this is a far smaller proportional figure than that for any other book-review medium, it is not a discredit to the *Times*.

The paper's policy is to review books chiefly of wide rather than limited public interest. Most textbooks and highly specialized, scholarly volumes get little or no attention, a practice that annoys some readers, who point to the regular space allotted mysteries, westerns, and juveniles and declare that this keeps out consideration of certain significant books.

The decision about what the *Book Review* is to deal with is left eventually to the section's editor, who is responsible only to the Sunday editor of the paper. The procedure for handling books prior to his moment of decision is efficient. Two 3″ x 5″ cards are made out for each volume. One is headed by the author's name, the other by the book title. These are put in a temporary file and then in a permanent file after the review has appeared, so that final data about the publication of the criticism may be included. The books are previewed by a corps of five staffers, each handling one or more specialties. The previewer types his summary and recommendations for reviewers on a standard form that goes to the editor.

The *Times* need not request books from publishers, as must many smaller papers and magazines. Publishers are so eager for reviews that sometimes they send unbound copies well in advance of publication (although they usually send completed volumes), replacing these later with finished books. These virtual page proofs of forthcoming publications are sent in turn to reviewers.

With a book to be reviewed, whether bound or unbound, the *Book Review* office sends an indication of desired length and deadline. The *Times'* critical writers are expected to know its style from reading the supplement and to be professional enough to know how to prepare copy properly. Occasionally a reviewer who is new to the *Times* is sent a telegram asking him if he will handle a particular book.

The selection of reviewers is on the basis of authority: the expert in a field is chosen for a nonfiction book; a novelist reviews novels; biographers handle biographies, and so on. This practice sometimes produces a review of the type known as logrolling (you praise my book and I'll praise your book) or breaks open long-standing disagreement between experts in the same field.

The *Times* is sensitive about revealing its rate of payment to its reviewers, but one is given to understand that it is adequate. The *Times'* reviewers whom this writer knows have all been better paid than those for any other publication within his knowledge. The *Book Review* staff is under American Newspaper Guild contract. Cartoons about the literary life, the publication has announced, will bring $50 each. A full-length critical article, according to unofficial reports, earns $250 or more. Ten cents a word evidently is no uncommon rate for a book review.

Production is the responsibility of a regular staff member. Another staffer first edits all copy, the production man plans layouts and make-up, a third carries out the plans. Two of the four women staff members (not counting the two secretaries) handle all pictures and other illustrations. One is completely responsible for a given issue; the other works on the following issue, so that one picture editor gives complete attention to the art work for each *Book Review.* Photographs come free from publishers or are bought from picture services and free lancers (as are cartoons) and are available, as well, in the *Times'* huge picture library.

Special critical articles are provided principally by regular staff members or by the *Times'* correspondents all over the world. For instance, A. M. Rosenthal, while resident correspondent in India, interviewed R. K. Narayan, a noted south Indian novelist, about his work in time for the article to be sent by cable and run on the same page with a review of Narayan's new book. The review was written in the United States. The *Book Review* is willing to consider special articles from free lancers but rarely publishes them, for they do not often fit the supplement's program or interests. Foreign correspondence, in addition to critical articles about authors and features, provides general coverage of literature in other countries. Foreign books are not often reviewed individually.

Advertising for the *Book Review* is solicited by several persons in the paper's general advertising offices who more or less specialize in *Book Review* accounts. Many of these advertisers, including the old-line publishers, have been buying space in the supplement for many years. One *Times* man put it: "much of their work could almost be set up automatically. Their stuff rolls in, week after week, sometimes one-half page, sometimes a full one, and that's that."

The Herald Tribune "Books"

Books, the supplement to the New York *Herald Tribune,* while produced under a plan that could be the envy of most literary editors, is not quite the paradise for critics to be found at the *Times.* However it is far more elaborate than all newspaper literary sections, except that of the *Times* and the Chicago *Tribune*. Like the latter's *Magazine of Books,* it shares some of its space with other subjects, mainly art.

Mrs. Irita Van Doren, literary editor of the *Herald Tribune,* has a staff of five, several doing mainly routine office work. Systematic records are kept, books are sent to more or less regular reviewers, and standards are high in all phases of the work. *Books* receives about 4,000 of the volumes published annually in this country, reviews 2,000, has an independent distribution of 20,000 a week, and has a distribution with the Sunday edition of the paper of 529,715.

Begun in 1924, its first editor was the noted critic and author, Stuart Sherman. Mrs. Van Doren, then his assistant, has been the only other editor since his death. It pays three cents a word for a review of a piece of fiction and four cents for one of a nonfiction volume. This supplement obtains copy from the *Herald Tribune*'s correspondents overseas by air mail.

The Critical Journals

If the writer of journalistic criticism is to see his material in print, he must know how to gain entry to the publications that publish his type of copy. It follows that he must know something about the publications themselves. One of the most important groups for him are the periodicals known as critical journals. This old-fashioned term is being used broadly here to include any magazine publishing considerable quantities of critical writing.

The American critical journal came originally, as did all our first journalism, from European models, particularly those of Great Britain. Some of the characteristics—if not the actual publications—of the earliest have survived. They have become identified in the public mind, and not always justly, with all of the periodicals. These characteristics are stodginess, dullness, parochialism, scholarliness, sobriety, and small circulations.

Few publications devoted entirely to criticism have lived more than a year or so. Without subsidy, life is impossible for them in a nation dominated, as is ours, by citizens as yet unprepared to take much interest in the critical appraisal and appreciation of the arts, with the exception of a few of the more popular forms.

The creator of critical journalism, therefore, finds that the major outlets for his work are the publications devoted either to many other subjects or those that must share space with noncritical aspects of the art in question. The music critic, for instance, can publish occasionally in *Harper's, The Atlantic, The Nation,* and a few others. Fore and aft his article in one of these magazines he is likely to find pieces on penology and power politics. He can more often publish his criticism in *Musical Quarterly, Musical*

Courier, Musical America, or one of the others specializing in his field. But when he does, what surrounds his contribution is likely to be news of the music world or a personality sketch of a musician. The periodical devoted solely to criticism died in the century before this, when journalism was a less costly enterprise.

America is a graveyard for periodicals that tried to exist on the offerings of critical writing. *World* (1847–52) may have been the first. Another, especially in its early years, was *The Literary Era* (1892–1905). *Book Culture,* a five-cent monthly, and *Impressions,* first a monthly and then a quarterly (the usual hint of loss of blood) each lasted only a few years after the turn of the century. The most famous of all that died, *The Bookman,* took only four of forty years of life (1895–1933) to shift from being a strictly literary journal to one of broader interests. Its subtitles reflected that shift. From its first year to 1899 it called itself "An Illustrated Literary Journal." But in the latter year this was changed to "A Review of Books and Life."

A Symbol of Events

The Saturday Review of today is symbolic of what has happened. Founded in 1924 as *The Saturday Review of Literature* by Christopher Morley, William Rose Benét, and Henry Seidel Canby, it grew out of the *Literary Review,* the weekly tabloid supplement of the New York *Evening Post.* It gained a respected but small place as a serious critical journal containing book reviews and critical articles on literature. Its circulation from 1924 to 1942 was small, although it had such distinguished editors as Canby, Bernard De Voto, and George Stevens.

When another capable journalist, Norman Cousins, took over as editor in 1942, he for a time continued the magazine largely as a journal of literary criticism. But it was evident that the mounting cost of production and the lack of advertising, needed to supplement circulation revenue, somehow had to be offset. About 1950, consequently, he began broadening the content and in 1952 dropped the words, *of Literature,* from the title. By 1959 the magazine had achieved a circulation of 200,000, and was offering regular sections on business, science, music, travel, and other topics, most of which were hardly literary and rarely dealt with through critical writing. It continued, however, to cover important books and publish much significant literary, music, television, and other criticism.

Exclusive devotion to literary criticism in journalistic form survives only in the New York *Times Book Review*. The New York *Herald Tribune Books* no longer is devoted wholly to literature, for the art and recordings departments also use space for their news and criticism. But both, as well as *Magazine of Books*, the Chicago *Tribune*'s supplement (which is printed in color, unlike the other two, and includes philately) are chiefly receptacles of critical writing. Whether they would remain so if published and distributed completely independently is unlikely. Another but tinier survivor in the realm of almost complete critical content is *Critical Digest*, a New York drama newsletter, which summarizes the news of and critical reaction to the new plays but publishes little critical material of its own.

Unusual in its own field of the motion picture is a pocket-size magazine of about 5,000 circulation called *Films in Review*. Published in New York, it is receptive to critical articles on this art, and announces on its cover that it publishes "honest reviews," thus reflecting a common opinion about the cinema criticism to be found in the fan magazines and general newspapers.

The "Little" Magazines

The "little" magazines and the scholarly quarterlies are familiar to only a small proportion of the general public. Yet they are important repositories of the critical writing of our time, since they are read by persons of influence: writers, teachers, and other intellectual leaders. They are so limited in distribution that it is wise to qualify this by saying that they are important in the long run, for they have little immediate impact and are largely unknown even to some serious critical writers.

Among the better-established "little" magazines of general literary content (so called because of small-size circulation and often few pages and small format) are *Accent*, *Epoch*, and *Prairie Schooner*. Scores of others, less regular in publication than these, also appear from time to time, many of them containing verse and criticism of poetry only. Among these several have had from a decade to a quarter of a century or more of life. The better-known ones are called *Driftwind, Beloit Poetry Journal, Kaleidograph, Poet Lore,* and *Wings.*

Although their circulations may run only into the hundreds or a few thousands, they have given encouragement to many poets and critics of poetry. Editors of the larger magazines, alert for new talent, watch them. One of the most famous discoveries in the field of fiction was Ernest Hemingway, whose early work was seen in *The Double Dealer* by a large New York book publishing house; this firm later published his first book.

The Quarterlies

Under the designation of quarterlies is a group of publications, some of which actually are monthlies, that have larger circulations than most of the "little" magazines, are subsidized usually by universities, and are enthusiastically hospitable to critical writing on all of the arts. Those that have made some impress on a relatively small public (but larger than the readership of the "little" magazines) include *The Antioch Review,* the *South Atlantic Quarterly, Sewanee Review,* the *Virginia Quarterly, Yale Review, Hudson Review, Kenyon Review, New Mexico Quarterly Review, Partisan Review,* and *American Scholar.*

None of these is devoted entirely to criticism. All use much of their space for literature itself and each has generous critical sections.[1] The criticism that is printed by several of them sometimes becomes criticism of criticism of criticism. Others have strong regional leanings, obvious from their titles (*Colorado Quarterly, Chicago Review*), and give preference, naturally, to critical writing that deals with the work of artists in the publication's geographical area.

In between the "little" magazines and the quarterlies is *Poetry: A Magazine of Verse,* a monthly which has managed to survive

---

[1] Granville Hicks, analyzing the autumn issues of *Sewanee, Partisan, Kenyon,* and *Hudson Reviews* in 1957, found that of the 605 pages, 391 were "for the critics."

and is generally regarded as a leading magazine of poetry. It carries extensive reviews of books of verse, often of those which the large media choose to ignore because of lack of public interest.

Thus in the United States the term *critical journal* in reality now means the magazines (and a few publications of similar content but newspaper format) that give major space to critical writing but are not totally devoted to it.

How to Find Them

One reason that more writers of journalistic criticism do not submit their material to the appropriate journals is that these publications are difficult to see or even find listed. Periodicals that do not carry advertising or sell only a miniscule amount of space are not recorded in most standard commercial guides. The names of the tiny, obscure "little" magazines are not in any easily obtainable directory, for neither do they carry any or much advertising nor are they issued with sufficient regularity to be dependably itemized in the standard market guides.

Most critical journals have no newsstand distribution; some are received by metropolitan and college libraries. A critical writer, especially one who specializes in a particular field, is wise therefore to subscribe to and hoard those he hopes to write for. He has less trouble, however, keeping an eye on the magazines that Dr. Frank Luther Mott, the noted historian of American magazines, says were for many years called "general literary monthlies." The survivors of this group, once made up of *The American Mercury, Harper's, The Atlantic, Scribner's, The Bookman, The Century,* and the *North American Review,* are only the first three, and the *Mercury* has changed its character sharply. The other two have been joined by *The Saturday Review* and *The Reporter,* neither of which is a monthly but both of which in content are not unlike the survivors. *The New Yorker* belongs here, as far as its critical content is concerned.

Information about their manuscript needs, rates of payment, and other data of particular interest to an aspiring contributor must be obtained through reference books and writers' periodicals. A few of the scholarly journals have prepared leaflets giving such information, which are available free on request and sometimes accompany a rejection slip.

Writers find it useful to acquaint themselves with as many of the following sources of information as possible:

BOOKS

Writer's Market. An annual market guide for creators of all kinds of material for books, magazines, newspapers, and other media. Edited by Aron M. Mathieu and Joseph A. Alvarez. Published by *Writer's Digest*, 22 E. 12th Street, Cincinnati 10, Ohio.

Writer's Handbook. Similar to the above, but with more essays on writing. Edited by A. S. Burack at 8 Arlington Street, Boston 16, Mass. Issued irregularly.

Directory of Newspapers and Periodicals. An annual record of publications useful chiefly to verify the existence of a publication and its address. Issued by N. W. Ayer & Son, Inc., West Washington Square, Philadelphia 6, Pa.

Ulrich's Periodicals Directory. The only world-wide list in English, it describes magazines but does not give rates to authors or manuscript needs. Revised about every five years. Eileen C. Graves, editor. R. R. Bowker Company, 62 W. 45th Street, New York 36, N. Y.

Literary Market Place. Subtitled "The Business Directory of American Book Publishing," this annual also lists information unavailable elsewhere: the names and addresses of newspaper, magazine, and syndicate critics. Edited by Anne J. Richter, published by R. R. Bowker Company, 62 W. 45th Street, New York 36, N. Y.

Editor & Publisher International Year Book. A supplement to the weekly trade magazine, *Editor & Publisher*, it lists daily newspaper critics and basic facts about dailies, but is not a writer's guide. Times Tower, New York 36, N. Y.

Standard Rate and Data Service, Inc. A series of magazine-like publications is issued by this firm, listing basic facts for use by potential advertisers; included are general consumer periodicals. Published at 1740 Ridge Avenue, Evanston, Ill.

Market guide information also is obtainable from certain textbooks on article writing, such as *Article Writing and Marketing* by George L. Bird (Rinehart, New York, 1956). But this must be checked against a later source, for changes have occurred in many of the smaller publications' editorships and addresses.

MAGAZINES

A few magazines for writers regularly announce the needs of publications that use critical journalism. Several print at regular intervals lists that serve as excellent checks on the annual compilations.

The Writer. Most issues contain a special list of periodicals and papers; usually these are available later by reprint. Typical is one called "Radio, TV, and Drama." Each month, also, there appears the section, "Where to Sell Manuscripts." Edited by A. S. Burack, 8 Arlington Street, Boston 16, Mass.

Author and Journalist. Also carries market data and annual lists that appear on special subjects, obtainable by buying back issues. In recent years such lists have covered the "little," poetry, and specialized magazines. Each July appears the "Midyear Market Guide" or "Handy Market List." Edited by Nelson Antrim Crawford, 1313 National Bank of Topeka Building, Topeka, Kans.

Writer's Digest. A monthly, it is similar to the other two magazines for writers, but emphasizes somewhat less the market lists on special subjects; instead it offers reports from cities, chiefly New York, on editorial needs. R. K. Abbott, editor, 22 E. 12th Street, Cincinnati 10, Ohio.

These are the big three of this type of aid. Others that may be helpful are *Writers Newsletter*, P. O. Box 251, Madison Square Garden, New York 10, N. Y., and *Rewrite*, 50 West Street, Lunenburg, Mass.

Trace is a quarterly published in England to keep track of the "little" magazines. Edited in America, however, by James Boyer May, P. O. Box 1068, Hollywood 28, Calif. It has little market data but contains an invaluable annual directory.

Publishers' Weekly, although intended for the book trade, carries all important news relating to magazines and newspapers that devote space to literary criticism, such as deaths of editors and changes in policies relating to book reviewing. R. R. Bowker Company, 62 W. 45th Street, New York 36, N. Y.

Magazine Industry Newsletter, a weekly "inside dope" sheet for magazine business executives, records internal news of the magazine world. Edited by Roy Quinlan at 40 E. 49th Street, New York 17, N. Y.

Magazines and books similar to these American guides also are published in a few foreign countries; facts about certain of the magazines are available in *Ulrich's Periodicals Directory.*

Selected Bibliography

Most of the book titles below deal entirely with critical writing, but not necessarily only the journalistic uses of it. If the reader is a novice in journalism he also should read some of the basic texts on journalism, especially those on reporting and journalistic writing techniques. The "Bibliography on Journalism" in the *International Year Book* number of *Editor & Publisher* magazine or the book, *The Journalist's Bookshelf*, published by Quill and Scroll Foundation, State University of Iowa, both offer lists of such texts.

A bibliography on the various arts is to be found in *Subject Guide to Books in Print* by Herbert B. Anstaedtt and Sara L. Prakken, published by Bowker, New York. This is a yearly index to the *Publishers' Trade List Annual*. See in it the section on bibliographies and on each of the fine and popular arts.

The richest parts of the bibliography below are those devoted to book and literary criticism, criticism in general, and dramatic criticism. It is not possible to classify all books accurately. For instance, Dr. Frank Luther Mott's valuable four-volume *History of American Magazines* contains much information about various kinds of criticism and might rightly be mentioned under book, drama, art, and music criticism separately.

This listing, although selective, also should make obvious that much research and descriptive writing are needed about such neglected subjects for criticism as art, dance, music, architecture, radio, television, photography, and motion pictures. Articles, some of them important to be sure, have appeared about all these subjects but they are not easily accessible, so that treatment in book form is greatly needed.

CRITICISM IN GENERAL

Brownell, W. C.: *Criticism*. New York, Scribner's, 1914.

Eliot, T. S.: *The Frontiers of Criticism*. Minneapolis, University of Minnesota, 1956.

Foerster, Norman: *Toward Standards*. New York, Farrar & Rinehart, 1930.

Grabo, Carl: *The Creative Critic*. Chicago, University of Chicago Press, 1948.

Greene, Theodore Meyer: *The Arts and the Art of Criticism*. Princeton, Princeton University Press, 1940.

Macy, John: *The Critical Game*. New York, Boni & Liveright, 1922.

Matthiessen, Francis O.: *The Responsibilities of the Critic*. New York and London, Oxford University Press, 1952.

Morris, Bertram: *The Aesthetic Process*. Evanston, Illinois, Northwestern University, 1943.

Mott, Frank Luther: *A History of American Magazines*, Cambridge, Harvard University Press, 1938, Vols. I, II, III. Cambridge, Belnap Press, 1957, Vol. IV.

Pepper, Stephen C.: *The Basis of Criticism in the Arts*. Cambridge, Harvard University Press, 1945.

Shaw, Theodore L.: *Precious Rubbish*. Boston, Stuart Art Gallery, 1956.

Smith, S. Stevenson: *The Craft of the Critic*. New York, Crowell, 1931.

ART

Venturi, Lionel: *The History of Art Criticism*. New York, Dutton, 1936.

BOOK AND LITERARY

Bennett, Arnold: *The Truth About an Author*. New York, Doran, 1911.

Buck, Philo: *Literary Criticism*. New York, Harper, 1930.

Drewry, John E.: *Book Reviewing*. Boston, *The Writer*, 1945.

Edgett, Edwin Francis: *I Speak for Myself*. New York, Macmillan, 1940.

Freund, Philip: *How to Become a Literary Critic.* New York, Beechurst Press, 1947.

Gard, Wayne: *Book Reviewing.* New York, Knopf, 1927.

Graham, Walter: *English Literary Periodicals.* New York, Nelson, 1930.

Hackett, Francis: *On Judging Books in General and in Particular.* New York, John Day, 1947.

Johnson, Charles F.: *Elements of Literary Criticism.* New York, Harper, 1898.

Jones, Llewellyn: *How to Criticize Books.* New York, Norton, 1928.

Mallory, Herbert S., Editor: *Backgrounds of Book Reviewing.* Ann Arbor, Michigan, Wahr, 1931, Rev.

Nitchie, Elizabeth: *The Criticism of Literature.* New York, Macmillan, 1929.

Peyre, Henri: *Writers and Their Critics.* Ithaca, Cornell University Press, 1929.

Sheehan, Donald: *This Was Publishing.* Bloomington, Indiana University Press, 1952.

Speller, Robert E., Thorp, Willard, Johnson, Thomas H., and Canby, Henry Seidel, Editors: *Literary History of the United States.* New York, Macmillan, 1955.

DANCE

Buckle, Richard: *The Adventures of a Ballet Critic.* London, Cresset Press, 1953.

DRAMA

Clapp, Henry Austin: *Reminscences of a Dramatic Critic.* Boston and New York, Houghton Mifflin, 1902.

Frick, Constance: *The Dramatic Criticism of George Jean Nathan.* Ithaca, Cornell University Press, 1943.

Fry, Christopher, Editor: *An Experience of Critics and the Approach to Dramatic Criticism.* New York, Knopf, 1953.

Hamilton, Clayton: *The Theory of the Theatre and Other Principles of Dramatic Criticism.* New York, Holt, 1939.

Littlewood, S. R.: *The Art of Dramatic Criticism.* London, Pitman, 1952.

Nathan, George Jean: *Testament of a Critic.* New York, Knopf, 1931.

Shaw, George Bernard: *Advice to a Young Critic and Other Letters.* New York, Crown, 1955.

LITERARY (*see* BOOK)

MOTION PICTURE

Dale, Edgar: *How to Appreciate Motion Pictures.* New York, Macmillan, 1938.

MUSIC

Biancolli, Louis: *The Flagstad Manuscript.* New York, Putnam's, 1952.

Calvocoressi, Michael D.: *The Principles and Methods of Musical Criticism.* London, Oxford University Press, 1931.

Graf, Max: *Composer and Critic: Two Hundred Years of Musical Criticism.* New York, Witmark, 1934.

Kastendieck, Miles, Editor: *Summary of Music Critics Workshops, 1953–1956.* Charleston, West Virginia, American Symphony Orchestra League, 1957.

Thompson, Oscar: *Practical Musical Criticism.* New York, Witmark, 1934.

Index

Abell, Arthur, 64
Accent, 191
Adams, J. Donald, quoted, 25, 81–82; 134, 185
Advertising and criticism, 21–22, 125, 176 ff.
Agate, James, 68
Allen, Steve, quoted, 29–30
American Mercury, The, 193
American Newspaper Guild, 47, 49
American Scholar, 192
American Symphony Orchestra League, 47
Antioch Review, The, 192
Apikian, Nevart, x, 16, 41–42
Architecture, criticism of, 109
Arnold, Matthew, 1; quoted, 74
Articles, critical:
    defined, 131–132
    sources of, 137
    writing of, 132
Associated Press, 168
Atkinson, J. Brooks, 26, 40–41
Atlantic, The, 21, 189, 193
Author and Journalist, 195
Authoritarian criticism, 75 ff.
Authoritarian critics, 75 ff.
Authors League of America, 47
Avery, Carolyn Jane, x

Babbitt, Irving, 80, 84
Barkham, John, 165
Barzun, Jacques, quoted, 68, 124
Bass, Milton R., x; quoted, 42–43; 64; quoted, 117; 163–164
Beatty, Richard C., 64
Beaumont, Cyril, 99
Beloit Poetry Journal, 192
Bennett, Arnold, quoted, 37; 109
Berenson, Bernard, 65
Berkvist, Robert, x
Bernays, Edward L., 31
Bernstein, Leonard, quoted, 43
Bird, George L., 132, 195
Birmingham, Frederic, quoted, 94
Book Culture, 190
Bookman, The, 190, 193
Books, 187, 191
Books:
    criticism of, 109 ff.
    useful in marketing manuscripts, 194
Borowski, Felix, 64
Brennecke, Ernest, Jr., quoted, 132
Brickell, Herschel, quoted, 28
Brittain, Vera, quoted, 92
Brown, Francis, 185
Brown, Ivor, quoted, 66
Brown, John Mason, 50, 133, 137
Brownell, Baker, 6

Brownell, W. C., 68, 78, 80
Bryant, William E., 58
Buckle, Richard, quoted, 99
Buckley, William F., Jr., quoted, 46
Bulliet, C. J., 59
Butcher, Fanny, 60
Butler, Samuel, quoted, 91–92

Callaway, Claude, x
Canby, Edward Tatnall, quoted, 125
Carty, James W., Jr., x
Cassidy, Claudia, 59
Century, The, 193
Chapman, John, 47
Chase, Edna Woolman, quoted, 121
Chase, Ilka, quoted, 121
Chicago *Evening Post,* 22
Chicago Review, 192
Chicago *Tribune,* 31, 32, 48–49, 119, 188
Chotzinoff, Samuel, 51, 98, 119
Christian Science Monitor art-music-theater page, insert in Chap. 11
Clark, Donald Lemen, quoted, 132
Clurman, Harold, 49, 91
Colorado Quarterly, 192
Columbia Missourian, reviews in, 167
Columbia (S. C.) *State* book-music-art page, insert in Chap. 11
Commonweal, The, 34
Composition, types of, 5
Conrad, Joseph, quoted, 28
Cook, Fred J., 46
Copperud, Roy H., 61
Copy, preparation of, 104 ff.
Cousins, Norman, quoted, 77; 190

Cowley, Malcolm, quoted, 27; 135
Critical articles:
    defined, 131–132
    sources of, 137
    writing of, 132
Critical attitudes, 81 ff.
Critical Digest, 191
Critical thinking, 5 ff.
Critical writers, number of, 13 ff.
Critical writing, *defined,* 3–4
Criticism:
    Anatole France's definition of, 75, 77
    and advertising, 21–22, 125, 176 ff.
    of architecture, 109
    authoritarian, 75 ff.
    of books, 109 ff.
    of the dance, 111 ff.
    of the drama, 113 ff.
    and humor, 94–95
    impressionistic, 75 ff.
    in magazines, 17
    of motion pictures, 115 ff.
    of music, 118 ff.
    of painting, 120 ff.
    of photography, 123–124
    and politics, 84
    and promotion, 21, 125, 169
    as promotion, 34
    of radio, 126 ff.
    of recordings, 124 ff.
    restraints upon, 21 ff.
    and reviewing, 7 ff.
    of sculpture, 120 ff.
    of television, 126 ff.
    theories of, 73 ff.
    and thinking, 130-131
    tone of, 93 ff.
Critics:
    authoritarian, 75 ff.
    freedom of expression for, 44 ff.

Critics—(*Continued*):
impressionistic, 75 ff.
influence of, 50 ff.
organizations of, 47
pressures on, 46
salaries of, 48–49
Crosby, John, 35, 52, 61
Crowther, Bosley, quoted, 101

Dale, Edgar, quoted, 78–79
Dance, criticism of, 111 ff.
Darrach, Brad, Jr., 60
Deschin, Jacob, quoted, 123
DeVoto, Bernard, quoted, 147
Discourse, forms of, 92–93
Disraeli, quoted, 2
Dolbier, Maurice, 26, 64
Double Dealer, The, 192
Downes, Olin, 49, 51, 98, 119
Drama, criticism of, 113 ff.
Dreiser, Theodore, 93
Driftwind, 192
Driver, Tom F., quoted, 96–97,
116
DuBois, William, 185
Duval, Anne Marie, x; quoted,
94

Edgett, Edwin F., 49, 58
Eliot, T. S., quoted, 37, 84
Epoch, 191
Ewald, William, quoted, 172–
173

Fadiman, Clifton, 32, 49, 91
Films in Review, 191
Flagstad, Kirsten, 51
Fleming, William, 16; quoted,
118, 119
Foerster, Norman, quoted, 71
France, Anatole, quoted, 75; 77
Frankenstein, Alfred, quoted,
10–11
Frazier, Carlton, x

Freeman, Donald, x, 127; quoted,
127; 128, 165
French, John C., 92
Fry, Christopher, quoted, 65
Funke, Lewis, 41

Gard, Wayne, quoted, 76
Gardiner, Harold C., quoted,
footnote 83
Gardner, Hy, quoted, 29–30
Garland, Robert, 60
Getlein, Frank, 33
Gibbs, Wolcott, 50, 59
Gilman, Lawrence, 51, 98
Gould, Edward S., quoted, 26
Gould, Jack, 35, 52–53, 61
Grabo, Carl, quoted, ix, 88
Gross, Ben, 52
Guernsey, Otis, 47

Hackett, Francis, 50
Haggin, B. H., 164
Hapgood, Norman, quoted, 26
Harman, Carter, 63, 118
Harper's, 21, 189, 193
Harrington, Harry F., quoted,
130–131
Harris, Sydney J., quoted, 97
Hatch, Robert, 164
Henderson, W. J., 51, 97–98
Hicks, Granville, 24; quoted, 25;
50, footnote 192
Hieronymous, Clara, 60
Hobson, Wilder, 63
Hochstein, Mort, x
Hogan, William, 60
Hope-Wallace, Philip, 66
Howells, W. D., 1
Hudson Review, 192
Hume, Paul, 84

Impressionistic criticism, 75 ff.
Impressionistic critics, 75
Impressions, 190

International Association of Art Critics, 47

Jackson, Joseph Henry, 60
Jarrell, Randall, quoted, 81
Jenks, Francis H., 58
Jensen, Oliver, quoted, viii-ix
Johnson, Samuel, quoted, 91, 92
Jones, Llewellyn, v; quoted, 5–6; 49, 50; quoted, 95–96
Journalism, study of, 68–69

Kalb, Bernard, 32
Kaleidograph, 192
Kastendienk, Miles, 119
Kenyon Review, 192
Keown, Eric, 66
Kern, Janet, 52
Kerr, Walter, 26, 33, 47, 64, 137–138
Key, Donald D., x; quoted, 53; 64; quoted, 122
Koch, Vivienne, quoted, 35
Kolodin, Irving, 91, 166; quoted, 170–171
Kupferberg, Herbert, quoted, 8–9

Language, 86 ff.
Lardner, John, 135
Law, 106
Levin, Harry, 2
Liebling, A. J., 51
Lipton, Lawrence, 135
Literary Era, The, 190
Literary Review, 190
Little magazines, 191
Littlewood, S. R., quoted, 32–33
Lochner, Louis P., 82
Lowell, James Russell, quoted, 82

McCarthy, Mary, 135
Macy, John, 50
Magazine of Books, 188, 191

Magazines:
criticism in, 17
useful in marketing manuscripts, 195–196
Make-up, 182
Mann, William, 98
Manuscripts, marketing of, 193 ff.
Marks, Percy, quoted, 93
Marsh, Robert C., x; quoted, 67, 108, 148 ff., 153 ff.
Martin, John, 100
Martin, Lawrence, quoted, 130–131
Maugham, Somerset, quoted, 92
Mayer, Martin, quoted, 66, 67, 89; 135, quoted, 136
Meisler, Stanley, quoted, 38–39, 55, 90
Mencken, H. L., 34, 93
Mitgang, Herbert, 102
Modern Photography, 123
More, Paul Elmer, 78, 84
Morehouse, Ward, 39, 62–63
Motion pictures, criticism of, 115 ff.
Mott, Frank Luther, 26, 197
Mumford, Lewis, 109
Music:
criticism of, 118 ff.
editor, 4–5
Music Critics Association, 47
Music Critics Workshops, 47
Musical America, 190
Musical Courier, 189
Musical Quarterly, 189

Nathan, George Jean, quoted, 33, 44; 50, 60; quoted, 81, 93–94; 133
Nation, The, 34, 189
National Board of Review of Motion Pictures, Inc., 117
National Review, 34
New Leader, The, 34

New Mexico Quarterly Review,
192
New Republic, The, 33, 34
New York Drama Critics Circle,
47
New York *Evening Post,* 190
New York *Herald Tribune,* quot-
ed, 8 ff.; 10, 21, 187, 188
New York *Herald Tribune Books,*
187, 191
New York *Times,* 21, 123, 133,
188
New York *Times Book Review,*
16, 184 ff., 191
New Yorker, The, 31, 32, 94,
109, 172, 193
Newsweek, 31; quoted, 133
Nichols, Lewis, 185
North American Review, 193
Norton, Elliot, 43–44
Note-taking, 107

Oakes, John B., 46
O'Brian, Jack, 29, 52
O'Flaherty, Terrence, 52

Painting, criticism of, 120 ff.
Parker, Dorothy, quoted, 94
Parker, Theodore H., quoted, 28
Partisan Review, 35, 173, 192
Pasternak, Boris, 82
Patterson, William D., x; quoted,
166, 167
Peden, William, 167
Pepper, Stephen, quoted, 73–74
Perkins, Francis D., quoted, 9–
10; 51
Peyre, Henri, quoted, 70–71, 77,
79, 80, 82; 84; quoted, 96
Phoenix *Arizona Republic* book
and art page, insert in Chap.
11
Photography, criticism of, 123–
124

Poe, Edgar Allan, 26
Poet Lore, 192
Poetry: A Magazine of Verse,
192
Politics and criticism, 84
Poore, Charles, 101, 185
Popular Photography, 123
Poteet, Ewing, 46
Prairie Schooner, 191
Prescott, Orville, 101, 185
Progressive, The, 34
Promotion and criticism, 21, 125,
169
Publishers' Weekly, 195

Quarterlies, 192–193
Quiller-Couch, Arthur, quoted,
92
Quinlan, David, quoted, 114

Radio, criticism of, 126 ff.
Rascoe, Burton, 39, 57–58
Recordings, criticism of, 124 ff.
Reporter, The, 193
Reviewing and criticizing, 7 ff.
Reviews, form of, 100–101
Rewrite, 195
Riley, Ruth E., x; quoted, 111
Root, Robert W., x; quoted, 166
Rosenberg, Harold, 135
Rosenfeld, Isaac, 65
Rosenfield, John, 56–57
Rosenthal, A. M., 187
Ruark, Robert, quoted, 2

St. Louis *Post-Dispatch* book
page, insert in Chap. 11
Saintsbury, George, 1
San Francisco *Chronicle,* 184
Sanborn, Pitts, 98, 119
Sargeant, Winthrop, 51, 63, 91,
98, 164
Sasonkin, Manus, quoted, 111
Saturday Evening Post, The, 34

Saturday Review, The, 21, 31, 35, 37, 165, 179, 190, 193
Saturday Review Syndicate, 165–166
Schubert theaters, 43–44
Scribner's, 193
Sculpture, criticism of, 120 ff.
Seldes, Gilbert, 35, 57
Sensenderfer, Robert, 59–60
Sevareid, Eric, quoted, 126
Sewanee Review, 192
Shaffer, John C., 22
Shaw, George Bernard, 1, 50; quoted, 91; 93; quoted, 94
Shaw, Theodore L., quoted, 25–26
Sherman, Stuart, 84, 188
Sherman, Thomas B., 180
Simmons, Ernest J., quoted, 136
Simon, Henry, 119
Skouras, Spyros, quoted, 30–31
Smith, Evelyn E., x
Smith, Harrison, 165; quoted, 169–170
Smith, S. Stevenson, 65; quoted, 82, 93
Snow, C. P., 26
Society of Magazine Writers, 47
Sokolsky, Robert L., x; quoted, 127 ff.; 176, 179, 180
Sorenson, John H., x, (*cartoon*), 14
South Atlantic Quarterly, 192
Spear, Elaine Stryker, x
Steinbeck, John, quoted, 31
Stevenson, Robert Louis, 91
Stokes, Richard L., 59
Style, 2, Chap. 7
Sublette, Bob, 60
Sylvester, Robert, quoted, 50
Syracuse (N. Y.) *Post-Standard*, 16

Taylor, Deems, 49
Television, criticism of, 126 ff.
Temianka, Henri, quoted, 55
Thompson, Oscar, quoted, 24; 50; quoted, 89, 96, 97–98; 98, 119
Thompson, Ralph, quoted, 25, 28
Thomson, Virgil, 98, 119
Tiger's Eye, The, 84
Time, 31, 32, 94
Trace, 195
Treanor, Aline, Jean, x; quoted, 57
Trilling, Lionel, 2
Tripp, Frank E., quoted, 87
Turner, Marjorie, quoted, 116
T. V. Key, 174; quoted, 175
T. V. Scout, 174

United Press International, 168

Van Doren, Irita, 188
Van Horne, Harriet, 52, 60
Variety, 50
Virginia Quarterly Review, 192
Vocabulary, 86 ff.

Wagner, Geoffrey, quoted, 2
Waugh, Arthur, quoted, 26
Weekly newspapers, criticism in, 16
Wenning, T. H., 64
West, Anthony, quoted, 24; 135
Whittaker, James, 119
Wilbur, Susan, 109
Wilder, Billy, quoted, 94
Wilson, Edmund, 26, 91
Winchester, C. T., quoted, vii–viii, 77
Wings, 192
Wolseley, Roland E., quoted, 141 ff.
Woollcott, Alexander, 59, 63

World, 190
Writer, The, 195
Writer's Digest, 195
Writers Newsletter, 195

Yale Review, 192

Zabel, Morton Dauwen, quoted, 34